THE LABRADOR RETRIEVER

Become a better trainer with the K9 Professional Training Series

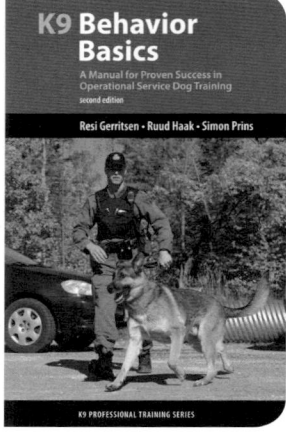
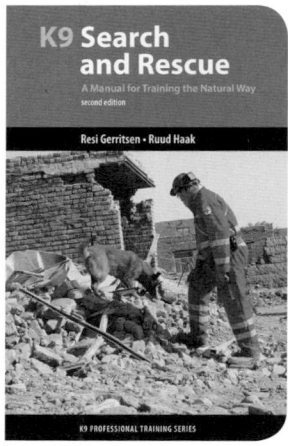

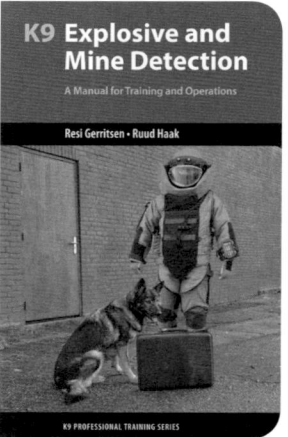

The K9 Professional Training Series teaches proven, effective, and positive training methods from highly experienced and respected trainers from Europe and North America. These uniquely authoritative manuals combine expert knowledge with detailed graphics and images.

See the complete list at

dogtrainingpress.com

THE LABRADOR RETRIEVER

From Hunting Dog to One of the World's Most Versatile Working Dogs

Dr. Resi Gerritsen
Ruud Haak

K9 PROFESSIONAL WORKING BREEDS SERIES

An imprint of
Brush Education Inc.

Copyright © 2021 Resi Gerritsen and Ruud Haak

21 22 23 24 25 5 4 3 2 1

Thank you for buying this book and for not copying, scanning, or distributing any part of it without permission. By respecting the spirit as well as the letter of copyright, you support authors and publishers, allowing them to continue to create and distribute the books you value.

Excerpts from this publication may be reproduced under license from Access Copyright, or with the express written permission of Brush Education Inc., or under license from a collective management organization in your territory. All rights are otherwise reserved, and no part of this publication may be reproduced, stored in a retrieval system, or transmitted in any form or by any means, electronic, mechanical, photocopying, digital copying, scanning, recording, or otherwise, except as specifically authorized.

Printed and manufactured in Canada

Brush Education Inc.
www.brusheducation.ca
contact@brusheducation.ca

Cover design: John Luckhurst; Cover image: Shutterstock ID 1057776890 (kphotograph)

Interior design: Carol Dragich, Dragich Design

Library and Archives Canada Cataloguing in Publication

Title: The labrador retriever : from hunting dog to one of the world's most versatile working dogs / Dr. Resi Gerritsen, Ruud Haak.
Names: Gerritsen, Resi, author. | Haak, Ruud, 1947- author.
Description: Series statement: K9 professional working breeds series | Includes bibliographical references.
Identifiers: Canadiana (print) 20210236469 | Canadiana (ebook) 20210236825 | ISBN 9781550598117 (softcover) | ISBN 9781550598124 (PDF) | ISBN 9781550598148 (EPUB)
Subjects: LCSH: Labrador retriever. | LCSH: Working dogs.
Classification: LCC SF429.L3 G47 2021 | DDC 636.752/7—dc23

Contents

    Introduction: The Six Retrievers vii
1. Origins of the Labrador Retriever 1
2. English Breeding 19
3. The Breed Standard 66
4. Training the Labrador Retriever 90
5. The Labrador Retriever as Hunting Dog 125
6. Other Training Possibilities for the Labrador Retriever 143
7. Health Care and Caring for the Older Dog 164
    Reading List 187
    Notes 193
    Photo Credits 196
    About the Authors 197

Introduction

The Six Retrievers

Retrievers were originally hunting dogs whose job was to collect game once the hunter shot it. That is, the different breeds of this type of gun dog were originally bred and trained to collect birds or other prey and bring it back to the hunter. Retrievers are trained to collect the game only if the hunter says that they may "run in"; until then, they must wait silently and observe where the game falls. To do their job well, retrievers must have a soft bite so they don't damage the game. They also must possess a great urge to please, learn, and obey.

Figure 0.1 The Labrador in its original task as a retrieving dog, here with a redhead duck (*Aythya americana*).

Today this combination of traits makes retrievers popular family dogs, and both the Labrador Retriever and the Golden Retriever are consistently found among lists of the top 10 best dogs for kids and families around the world. The retriever's willingness to please, patient nature, and trainability also contribute to the continuing popularity of the Labrador Retriever and Golden Retriever as working dogs for other tasks, such as search work for police and customs, search and rescue, and guide and other service work.

Figure 0.2 The modern Labrador Retriever.

Most popular retrievers
- Golden Retriever
- Labrador Retriever

Other retrievers
- Curly-Coated Retriever
- Flat-Coated Retriever
- Chesapeake Bay Retriever
- Nova Scotia Duck Tolling Retriever

Although we will focus on the Labrador Retriever in this book, it's worth taking a brief look at the other retriever breeds first to understand their similarities and differences.

Figure 0.3 Labrador Retriever.

Curly-Coated Retriever

The ancestor of the Labrador Retriever, the St. John's dog or Labrador dog, was crossed with other breeds and can therefore be regarded as the ancestor of other retrievers as well. The Curly-Coated Retriever resulted from crossing the St. John's dog with the water spaniel, and probably also the poodle. This crossing resulted in a black or liver-colored dog with — except for the head to mid-skull — a coat that consists of short, dense, slightly greasy curls. Curly-Coated Retrievers are good-natured, tough workers that are pleasant, intelligent, and of excellent use in hunting, especially for waterfowl.

Flat-Coated Retriever

From a cross between the Labrador dog and a setter, the Flat-Coated Retriever was born, a beautiful, elegant dog that for years was the best retriever in England. However, the breed suffered some damage due to World War I. At the start of the war, the breed was almost exclusively in the hands of gamekeepers, who were among the first people to volunteer in the army. After the gamekeepers left for war, their dogs were killed or were adopted

Figure 0.4 Curly-Coated Retriever.

Figure 0.5 Flat-Coated Retriever.

by people who did not breed them anymore. Fortunately, the breed was rescued and is now in good shape.

Chesapeake Bay Retriever

The Chesapeake Bay Retriever was born in the 19th century on the east coast of North America, near the site that gave the breed its name. Reportedly, the breed came to be after an English ship was wrecked in 1807 off the coast of Maryland. Along with the crew, two young dogs, either Newfoundlands or Labradors, were saved. The male, named Sailor, was reddish; the female, named Canton after the wrecked ship, was black. Their breeding with local dogs, including retrievers, resulted in the Chesapeake Bay Retriever.

The dog was so named because it was mainly used in the bay, which used to be full of ducks, thanks to the lush growth of wild celery and other plants. The "Ches" is an excellent hunting dog, especially for waterfowl, although it proved somewhat less manageable than other retrievers. The breed is particularly resistant

Figure 0.6 Chesapeake Bay Retriever.

to the cold. At the field trials of the American Chesapeake Club in 1935, when it was 6.8°F (−14°C), the winning dog swam for more than half an hour behind a fleeing duck before catching it. After shaking and rolling on its side, the dog was dry and ready to go again.

Nova Scotia Duck Tolling Retriever

The Nova Scotia Duck Tolling Retriever was bred in Nova Scotia in the early 19th century to toll (lure) and retrieve waterfowl. Their color includes various shades of red or orange with lighter featherings and underside of tail. They usually have at least one white marking on the tip of the tail or on the feet, chest, or blaze.

The way the dogs hunt is unique. The dog runs, jumps, and plays along the shoreline in full view of a flock of ducks, occasionally disappearing from sight and then quickly reappearing, aided by the hidden hunter, who throws sticks or a ball for the dog. Its playful actions arouse the curiosity of the ducks swimming offshore, and they are lured within gunshot range. The

Figure 0.7 Nova Scotia Duck Tolling Retriever.

Toller is subsequently sent out to retrieve the dead or wounded birds.

Golden Retriever

The Golden Retriever is a long-haired, sturdy dog that appears in all golden shades from light cream to dark gold. Presumably it originated from recessive "blond" Flat-Coated Retrievers, with crosses of the Irish Setter and yellow bloodhound. Originally, because of its excellent nose, the Golden Retriever was used as a hunting dog in the deer hunt. Nowadays it is a popular pet and often shown at exhibitions.

Figure 0.8 Golden Retriever.

Labrador Retriever

In 1991, the Labrador Retriever took first place as the most popular dog registered by the American Kennel Club. Into the 21st century, the Labrador continues to be among the most popular pets due to its great disposition and versatility. They are devoted family members as well as fine police search dogs. They

Figure 0.9 Labrador Retrievers are excellent working dogs, especially for nose work.

are good with children, tend to enjoy the company of other dogs, and are used as guide dogs, search and rescue dogs, and excellent K9s for all sorts of scent detection.

Everyone who works with a Labrador Retriever or wants to start working with one should become aware of the many possibilities this breed offers. *The Labrador Retriever* takes a look at the origin and history of the breed, as well as its outer appearance, senses, and inner drives and personality traits. With this understanding as a foundation, we then explore the many training possibilities for the breed, including, of course, its original task as a gun dog, but also its great suitability as a service and detector dog. We end with notes about the health concerns of the Labrador and a discussion about caring for older dogs, once their formal working days are behind them. Whether you know the breed well or are just exploring your options for a working dog, we hope this book will provide the information you need.

DISCLAIMER

While the contents of this book are based on substantial experience and expertise, working with dogs involves inherent risks, especially in dangerous settings and situations. Anyone using approaches described in this book does so entirely at their own risk and both the author and publisher disclaim any liability for any injuries or other damage that may be sustained.

1

Origins of the Labrador Retriever

The Labrador Retriever shares its great enjoyment of water with the Newfoundland dog. Both breeds were initially bred in what is now the Canadian province of Labrador and Newfoundland, from which they also got their names. The exact origins of the Newfoundland and Labrador are unclear. All that we know for certain is that both breeds were well established in the area by the late 17th century. They were bred separately, but were also crossbred with each other.

In the first part of the 19th century, both breeds were brought to England, where they entered a great prime period. Although the differences between the large, heavily coated Newfoundland dog and the smaller, short-haired Labrador Retriever were already evident, the records do not reveal which dogs came to England first.

Geographic Conditions

It is worth considering the climate in which the dogs originally lived and worked to better understand why they were bred for their particular set of physical and mental traits. Traditionally people lived by the sea and needed dogs that could work in cold water and withstand cool to cold temperatures on land. The island of Newfoundland, located in the Gulf of St. Lawrence, has a temperate marine climate. Winters are usually mild with a

Figure 1.1 Statues of a Newfoundland and a Labrador (at approximately 1.5 times life size), in Harbourside Park, St John's, Newfoundland.

Figure 1.2 Brown Newfoundland dog.

normal temperature of 32°F (0°C). Summer days range from cool to hot with a normal temperature of 60.8°F (16°C). The normal annual rainfall is 41 inches (105 cm) and the normal snowfall is 118 inches (300 cm).

Figure 1.3 Newfoundland and Labrador.

Labrador, on the Canadian mainland, has a polar, continental climate with summer temperatures not averaging above 60.8°F (16°C) and an average winter temperature of −3.2°F (-20°C). Labrador winters are much colder than those on Newfoundland. While summers are shorter and generally cooler, extreme high temperatures are not uncommon.

Dogs of Indigenous Peoples

The original inhabitants of Newfoundland and Labrador include both First Nations and Inuit peoples. Because the Inuit, especially, made excellent use of dogs for travel and transport, it might be reasonable to assume that Newfoundland and Labrador dogs are descended from Indigenous people's animals.

The Inuit people of Labrador traveled throughout the year, hunting the animals that were their source of food, clothing, tools, and shelter. In the summer, the people traveled over land by foot or they traveled on the water using kayaks. In the winter, they used a *komatik*, a large sled pulled by dogs. Brenda Clarke writes, "Dogs were an extremely important part of the economy. The Inuit depended on them not only for transportation, but also for help in the hunt and as an emergency food supply."[1]

Figure 1.4 A 1909 illustration of Inuit people and their dogs by Dr. Freiherr Ernst Stromer von Reichenbach. As a hunting companion, the Inuit dog's predatory skills helped stack the odds of locating and retrieving game in the hunters' favor. In a harsh environment where animals were almost the sole source of all that was needed to sustain life, the dogs were a critical part of Inuit life.

The British surgeon and cynologist John Henry Walsh (1810–1888) wrote about Inuit people's dogs:

> The dog ... is about 22 or 23 inches high, with a pointed fox-like muzzle, wide head, pricked ears and wolf-like aspect; the body is low and strong, and clothed with long hair, having an undercoat of thick wool; tail long, gently curved, and hairy; feet and legs strong and well formed; the colour is almost always a dark dun with slight disposition to brindle, and black nuzzle.[2]

The dogs from Labrador and Newfoundland that were imported to England in the early 19th century had hanging ears,

Origins of the Labrador Retriever

Figure 1.5 Labrador Dog, 1901.

only very rarely had curly tails, and didn't otherwise look like Nordic-type polar dogs. Therefore it is likely that the dogs exported to England were not Indigenous people's dog breeds, but were instead descended from dogs imported from Europe. Let's then take a look at the early European visitors to this region.

Viking Dogs

About 1000 CE, the first Europeans came to North America and formed a settlement at L'Anse aux Meadows, located on the northern tip of Newfoundland. These Vikings from Norway brought dogs to their settlement at "Vinland," as they called it. The Viking dogs were big and strong and bear resemblance to the Newfoundland dog. But the Norwegian settlement at Vinland was very small, probably not over 60 people, and it didn't exist for long before the Vikings moved on to other regions. That the dogs they brought resemble today's Newfoundland dog is likely more coincidence than an indication of genetic connection. The Viking settlement was short-lived, and there is no evidence that the Beothuk people, the earliest long-term inhabitants of Newfoundland, used dogs.

Fishing Dogs

After the Viking settlement disappeared, it was centuries before other Europeans explored the region. At the end of the 15th century, Portuguese explorers were the next to visit. One of them, João Fernandes Lavrador, sailed the coasts of Greenland and northeastern North America, including the peninsula that eventually took his name.

The English explorer John Cabot set foot ashore on Newfoundland on June 24, 1497, and claimed the island for England. After Cabot, Portuguese, Basque, Spanish, French, and English migratory fishers made regular visits. The fishers traveled to Newfoundland to fill their boats and returned to Europe to sell their catch, but they sometimes came ashore to dry their fish, replenish supplies, and trade with Indigenous people.

Figure 1.6 European explorers brought dogs with them. German woodcut engraved by J. A. Lonicer, 1582.

In 1501, Portuguese explorers charted part of the coast of Newfoundland in a failed attempt to find the Northwest Passage, a route to Asia. The first colonists to settle there called the island "Terra Nova," meaning "New Land" in Portuguese and Latin.

The Portuguese had dogs descended from an old Portuguese livestock guardian breed, which they called Cane di Castro Laboreiro, named after the village in northeastern Portugal where the yellow-brown dogs were found. In their homeland, the dogs lived in spartan conditions while defending livestock from wolves and bears, and Portuguese fishers brought the tough animals on their boats as protection from pirates and other dangers. It is believed that the brindle color that once existed in early retriever dogs came from this breed. Some suggest that the name "Labrador" comes from a misunderstanding or mishearing of the *Laboreiro* in the Portuguese dog's name.

Portuguese fishers also had a breed called Cão de Agua, a water dog that helped them by bringing in the fishing nets, retrieving articles swept overboard, and catching escaped fish. Both breeds had characteristics that are also found in today's Labrador Retrievers.

It's likely that early European dogs in Newfoundland were a motley crew. After all, the French and Spanish Basques used the island as a whaling and fishing ground, as did the Portuguese and, later, the French, Dutch, and English. All their various dogs were probably crossed, including poodle-type water dogs, spaniels, and herding dogs of all sorts. Out of this canine mix came the St. John's water dog, a breed that varied greatly in appearance.

English sailors to visit and explore the land most likely had dogs with them, as most sailors of that time did. In the opinion of Countess Howe, a well-known breeder of Labrador Retrievers, the English sailors probably brought St. Hubert Bloodhounds to Newfoundland:

> In England in those days, the black hounds of St. Hubert were much prized and it is well within the bounds of possibility that some of these dogs found their way to Labrador and Newfoundland and that they were the ancestors

VARIOUS RETRIEVERS.

CROSS -BETWEEN WATER SPANIEL AND NEWFOUNDLAND DOG—BETWEEN WATER SPANIEL AND SETTER DOG—BETWEEN SETTER AND NEWFOUNDLAND DOG.

Figure 1.7 Various retrievers from W. N. Hutchinson. *Dog Breaking, The Most Expeditious, Certain, and Easy Method*, 1869.

of the modern Labrador. It is doubtful if the real origin of the breed will ever be decisively settled, but it is certain that as the fishing industry increased in Labrador, a breed of dog was founded there that has become world-famous. It seems an established fact that there were two distinct types of this dog, a larger, stronger and long-haired dog and a lighter, smooth-coated variety. The larger, heavier dogs

Origins of the Labrador Retriever

Figure 1.8 A 1908 dog team that seems to include dogs of various breeds.

were used as draught animals to pull sleighs and generally make themselves useful. The lighter, smoother coated variety were taken by wildfowlers and fishermen and were used to retrieve game from rough seas, and also retrieve fish which would otherwise have escaped. Both these varieties found their way to these shores and attracted attention. They were known as Newfoundland dogs—which, of course, was confusing. Finally, about 1812–14, Colonel Peter Hawker sought to make the matter clearer and called the larger dog Newfoundland and the smaller the lesser Newfoundland, or the Labrador or St. John's dog, named for the harbour in Newfoundland where they were often seen.[3]

St. John's Water Dog

The first European inhabitants of the region lived, like the Indigenous people before them, mainly from fishing and hunting. For that work they had the Newfoundland dog and St. John's water dog, which had some similarities due to cross-breeding. Both varieties worked without regard for bad weather, were excellent swimmers, and were fond of water. Because of the similarities between both types of dog, it is impossible to say for sure at which place and time the modern Labrador came into being.

The St. John's water dog developed as a regional dog in Newfoundland, probably a mix of many types of dogs brought there by the Portuguese, English, and Basques. For example, the Basques could have brought several types of dogs to the island:
- the Pyrenean Shepherd
- the Perro de Agua Español, an old Spanish version of the water dog
- the Pyrenean Mastiff and the Great Pyrenees, livestock guardian mastiffs

Each of these could have played a role in development of the St. John's water dog. It's also certainly possible that Inuit people's dogs from Labrador were also included in the breed, but that is speculation. There are no records to say for sure.

In 1822, William Epps Cormack, a Newfoundland pioneer born in St John's, Newfoundland, became the first person of European descent to cross the interior of the island and explore along the southern coastline. In his account of his journey, he wrote that he saw Europeans along the coast using "small water dogs" that he described as "admirably trained as retrievers in fowling and [being] otherwise useful. The smooth or short-haired dog is preferred because in frosty weather, the long-haired kind become incumbered with ice on coming out of the water."[4] These "small water dogs" were undoubtedly St. John's water dogs.

Built for Cold

Of the special requirements of dogs that must work in cold water, Charles William George St. John, an English naturalist and sportsman, wrote the following in 1849:

> A dog who has much water-work to do should always be kept in good condition, and, if possible, even fat. It is a mistake to suppose that allowing him to come into the house and warm himself before the fire makes him less hardy; on the contrary, I consider that getting warm and comfortable before the kitchen fire on coming home gives the retriever a better

chance of keeping up his strength, health, and energy when much exposed to cold and wet during the day; a far better chance, indeed, than if, on returning, he is put into a cold kennel, where, however well supplied with straw, hours must elapse before he is thoroughly warm and dry. Most rough dogs stand cold well enough as long as they are tolerably dry, but frequent wetting is certain to cause disease and rheumatism. I am sure, too, with regard to water dogs, that a good covering of fat is a far more efficacious means of keeping them warm than the roughest coat of hair that dog ever wore. In wild animals, such as otters, seals, etc., which are much exposed to wet in cold countries, we always find that their chief defence against the cold consists in a thick coating of fat, and that their hair is short and close.

In like manner, dogs who are in good condition can better sustain the intense cold of the water than those whose only defence consists in a shaggy hide. Short-coated dogs are also the most active and powerful swimmers, and get dry sooner than those who are too rough-coated.[5]

Concurring with St. John's view, Scottie Westfall comments that both the Golden Retriever and Labrador Retriever "tend towards pudginess." However, he notes that "I don't think anyone is claiming that a fat dog is a healthy dog, but it does suggest that having slightly more body fat content might be an advantage for a water retriever." Furthermore, he states that the oily, dense coat of the Labrador has the "more functional coat than any of the feathered retrievers."[6]

Dogs in Newfoundland

Lambert de Boilieu visited Labrador from England in the early 1850s as a mercantile agent for an English company. He became intimately familiar with the hardworking water curs and their many uses, and he compiled his recollections in a book, *Recollections of Labrador Life*. His praise for the Labrador is today well known: "The Labrador dog, let me remark, is a bold fellow, and, when well taught, understands, almost as well as any

Figure 1.9 Billy, a St. John's water dog or Lesser Newfoundlander, from *The Dog in Health and Disease,* published in 1867. Curiously, the same illustration is used for Wyndham, the dog of Mr. R. Brailsford of Birmingham (UK), in the 1904 book *Hondenrassen* (Dog Breeds): Volume 1, Hunting Dogs.

Christian biped, what you say to him."[7] De Boilieu's admiration for the Labrador was extensive:

> During winter, for want of horses, dogs are used for the purpose of conveying all sorts of produce to and from the bays, as well as for pleasure. Some are trained as retrievers, watch, house, and water dogs. Still they are all of the same breed. The retriever is well known in England, but I fancy the duty of the Labrador watch-dog is little if at all understood. In the summer and fall, then, many stray ducks may be seen frequenting the small bays round the islands; the watch-dog lands with you, and, with much caution, examines the shore, and directly he observes ducks, he will instantly lie down and crawl out of their sight, then immediately rise and run towards you, when by his actions you may be sure he has

Figure 1.10 The book *Hondenrassen* (1904) included a drawing of Johnnie, described as a St. John's Dog or Labrador Dog, owned by Dr. Bond Moore from Wolverhampton (UK).

sighted a company. He leads the way, and when in the vicinity of the birds, down he crouches, and you must do the same.

Should you be over-eager, and fire at too great a distance, and miss your birds, the dog looks towards them for a moment, as if reflecting!—"It's no use going into the water, he has not killed any," and stands still. If, on the other hand, you have a good shot—killing, say, half-a-dozen, and crippling three or four—in he bounds, leaving the dead birds and giving chase to the cripples. If they are wounded in the wings they swim with difficulty, and cannot dive, and so become an easy spoil. The dog has the instinct to know this, for he wastes but little time in the pursuit. It constantly arises that the spot from whence the ducks are shot is, at least, ten feet perpendicular from the water; sportsmen provide themselves in such instances with what is termed a "gunning gaff," some twelve feet long, with an iron crook at the end, made in the shape of a shepherd's crook. The dog brings a duck one at a time under the rock; you place the crook round its neck, and draw it up or land it.

The last bird the dog retains in his mouth, and allows himself to be drawn up in a somewhat scientific manner; that is to say, having seized the bird firmly across the wings he swims under the rock, and allows his master to place the hook through his collar at the back of the neck; then placing his paws against the rock, and throwing his weight on the gaff, he gracefully walks up and lands his game … Of a fine day I have seen these dogs near the landwash amusing themselves fishing, diving six or seven feet, and bringing up a fish every time. Their mode of diving is not direct, but spiral.

It has been said a goose is a foolish bird, and certainly the geese of Labrador are very foolish indeed. They are found some miles up the bays, and when discovered the dog uses a simple artifice to decoy them. Near the shore (the

Figure 1.11 William Taplin, a British naturalist, wrote in 1803 that "The dog of Newfoundland in a state of purity, uncontaminated by the blood of any inferior race is one of the most majestic and awefully attracting of all the canine variety." Painting by Philip Reinagle, engraving by John Scott, in William Taplin's *Sportsman's Cabinet*, 1803.

neighbourhood of a small wood, with goose-grass in the foreground, is their favourite resort) he rushes out of the wood into the water and swims some eight or ten yards, with head low and-tail out — looking something like a water-fowl — then comes back to the shore, and so continues until he fancies they are within shot, when he quietly waits by your side watching your gun, and, by his looks, showing his anxiety to see the flash. Then off he goes and secures his birds, and lands them at your feet.

The house-dog has a peculiar sagacity. I trained one to keep house in a noiseless manner. If myself or steward was not at home, and a visitor called, the dog would allow him to walk in, sit down, light and smoke his pipe, as if unconscious of his presence; but if the visitor attempted to leave the house the

Figure 1.12 Hamilton Smith wrote 1840 about the dog of Newfoundland: "The true breed of this race is almost semi-palmated; and, consequently, they swim, dive, and endure the water better and longer than any other dog in existence." Drawing by Charles Hamilton Smith and engraving by William Home Lizars in William Jardine's *The Naturalist's Library*, 1840.

Figure 1.13 *Chien de Terre Neuve* (Newfoundland dog) from 1824. From Geoffroy Saint-Hilaire and Frédéric Cuvier, *Histoire Naturelle des Mammiferes* (Volume I).

dog was up in an instant, and, placing himself in the doorway, showed a set of teeth of dazzling but appalling whiteness. The frightened fellow again returns and takes his seat, the dog once more lies down, and thus the pair are seen on the return of one of the household. A visitor once served that way takes care to look through the window on his next call, to see if any one is at home.[8]

Shipped to England

Trade between Newfoundland and Labrador and England became more intensive in the early 19th century. The main commodity, codfish, was transported from St. John's, in Newfoundland, to Poole Harbour, in Dorset county, England. The first dogs from Newfoundland and Labrador came to England around 1800. They attracted attention because of their style of swimming and the pleasure with which they retrieved all manner of articles. English sportsmen were attracted to the dogs immediately and bought them for hunting. The English sportsmen, as it happens, had the luxury to breed a separate dog for every purpose. But with the dogs from Newfoundland and Labrador, they had a dog that by nature was a very good retriever *and* an excellent swimmer.

Yet although the dogs were exported from Newfoundland and Labrador to England, we see a difference in the animals developing on either side of the ocean. To the average British person, the word "Labrador" very often referred to a long-haired dog, but in Labrador and Newfoundland, it referred to a dog with an otter's coat. Scottie Westfall observes the following:

> Because the smooth coat is dominant to the feathered coat, one would have thought that the majority of retrievers in Britain would have been short-haired. That is not what we see. The feathered wavy-coated retriever was the most common retriever in Britain during the late nineteenth and early twentieth centuries. It is sometimes suggested that the feathering came from setters that were crossed with these dogs, but the simple rules of population genetics say that this is unlikely. If the smooth-coated dogs were bred to setters, the majority of the dogs that resulted from those crosses would have been short-haired. But that is not what the historical record shows.[9]

De Boilieu offers a reason the long-haired dogs were so dominant in England: "The dogs sent to England, with rough shaggy coats, are useless on the coast; the true-bred and serviceable dog having smooth, short hair, very close and compact to the body." As a mercantile agent in Labrador, De Boilieu knew what the people of Newfoundland and Labrador valued. In short, they kept the best, short-haired dogs for themselves and sent the long-haired animals for export. This is why the dogs of Newfoundland were mostly of the short-haired type.

Concerning the name of these dogs, a lot of confusion existed for a long time: the names Newfoundland, Lesser Newfoundland, Little Newfoundlanders, Newfoundland Water Dog, St. John's Dog, Black Water Dog, and later on also

Labrador Dog, Lesser Labrador, English Retriever, English Labrador, and Labrador Retriever were all used. But the fishers from Newfoundland didn't care what they were called. They continued to earn extra income from their dog business, selling the English sportsmen "original Newfoundland dogs."

2

English Breeding

Eventually the trade in "original Newfoundland dogs" from Newfoundland and Labrador to England increased so much that the quality of the dogs decreased. Little care was taken in breeding them — they had become merchandise more than carefully honed working tools. Thus, some English sportsmen decided to get the dogs themselves from the origin rather than using local British breeders. Colonel Peter Hawker was one of the first English sportsmen who, in the beginning of the 19th century, regularly traveled between England and Newfoundland. He imported many dogs and also gave a fine description of the Labrador. In his book *Instructions to Young Sportsmen,* written in 1814, Colonel Hawker describes the Labrador Retriever "as by far the best for every kind of shooting." He writes that the Labrador,

> Oftener black than of another colour, and scarcely bigger than a Pointer, … is made rather long in the head and nose, pretty deep in chest, very fine in the legs, has short or smooth hair, does not carry his tail so much curled as the other (Newfoundland) and is extremely quick in running, swimming and fighting, and their sense of smell is hardly to be credited.[1]

The first dogs Colonel Hawker imported went to the second Earl of Malmesbury (1778–1841), a passionate sportsman whose estate, Heron Court, was near Poole. Malmesbury started breeding the dogs, and his successor, the third Earl of Malmesbury (1807–1889), kept the Malmesbury lines going until his death.

Colonel Hawker's writings mention an increase in dogs being imported from Newfoundland and Labrador. Not all those dogs were purebred as we know the breed today, as can be seen in Figure 2.1.

The Buccleuch Line

At about the same time, in 1835, the fifth Duke of Buccleuch (1806–1884) started a kennel of St. John's dogs in Scotland.

Figure 2.1 This St. John's water dog, owned by Mr. Alsop, keeps watch over a package by the roadside. In the 19th century, the term "Labrador Dog" almost universally refers to the St. John's water dog in both its long-coated form, exported to England, and the smooth-coated form that the Newfoundlanders preferred. *Watchful Sentinel* (also named *Cora: A Labrador Dog*), by Sir Edward Landseer, 1823.

His brother Lord John Scott (1809–1860) and the tenth Earl of Home (1769–1841) were also impressed by the Labrador Retriever as a worker on land and in the water. They embarked on a similar, but independent breeding program. The three noblemen lived within a 30 mile (48 km) radius, and through their work, developed what became known as the Buccleuch line.

The eleventh Lord of Home (1799–1881) continued his predecessor's breeding program, but he stopped breeding toward the end of his life and the line was nearly extinct by the time of his death. However, a chance meeting changed that. The sixth Duke of Buccleuch and the twelfth Earl of Home were decided to participate in a water-fowl shoot on the south coast. There the two men were impressed by what the third Earl of Malmesbury's dogs, of the same bloodlines as their father's kennels, were capable of doing.

Malmesbury gave the two younger lords some of the dogs from his lines in 1885. And from these dogs, the Buccleuch line was revitalized. Two of the dogs were Ned (born 1882) and Avon (born 1885). Many say that these two dogs are the ancestors of all British Labs. Buccleuch Avon is said to have sired "liver-colored" pups, making him the likely ancestor of the chocolate gene carriers line. But that two different kennels (Buccleuch's and Home's), breeding independently for at least 50 years, had such similar dogs argues that the Labrador was kept very close to the original St. John's breed.

Some other breeders of the Labrador Retriever of that time tried to improve the breed by crossing them with the pointer, setter, harrier, and, of course, the Flat-Coated Retriever. Inbreeding with the Flat-Coated Retriever was especially popular because that breed was the best gun dog of the time. All these efforts were generally unsuccessful.

The timing of the change to the name Labrador Retriever from St. John's dog is unknown. It must have occurred sometime at the beginning of the 19th century, because in 1839, the fifth Duke of Buccleuch wrote a letter in which he reported that he took his "Labrador," Moss, with him when he went hunting in Naples, and the tenth Earl of Home, who traveled with him, was accompanied by his "Labrador," Drake.

By the middle of the 19th century, some noble families, such as the Duke of Buccleuch, the Earl of Malmesbury, and Sir Richard Graham (of Netherby Kennel), had built up a good strain of Labrador Retrievers. They began to keep a record of their breeding results in their kennels, and they tried to breed as purely as possible, with no outcrosses.

The Breed Goes into Decline at Its Origins

In Newfoundland in the mid-19th century, the dogs became threatened because Newfoundland's British governor wanted to encourage more sheep farming. To prevent any menace to sheep, he ordered that there could be no more than one dog per family. Later, in 1885, the Newfoundland Sheep Protection Act imposed a heavy license fee on dogs. Because there was a higher tax rate on females than males, many female pups were destroyed at birth, sending the breed into decline in the colony.

In 1895, the British Quarantine Act passed, which prohibited dogs from entering Great Britain without a license and without first undergoing a strict six-month quarantine. Britain did not yet have rabies and did not want to have it introduced, but the law made importing dogs into Britain next to impossible.

Breed Resurgence

Although these changes were hard on breeders in Newfoundland, the changes ultimately were good for the future of the breed, because British breeders were forced to breed their dogs pure. Some breeders, like the third Earl of Malmesbury, had already done so for a long time. As he wrote in 1887 in a letter to the sixth Duke of Buccleuch about his breeding line, "We always call mine Labrador dogs and I have kept the breed as pure as I could from the first I had from Poole."[2]

The truth of his words can be seen by comparing Landseer's painting from 1823 (Figure 2.1) with the earliest photograph of a Labrador Retriever, named Nell, from 1867 (Figure 2.2). Decades apart, the two dogs look almost the same.

Half a century later, breeders attached great value to the short-haired oily coat and otter tail, considering them two of the

ENGLISH BREEDING

Figure 2.2 Nell, a St. John's water dog, born about 1856. This is probably the earliest photo of a Labrador. Nell's white feet and a white muzzle were traits noted in other Labradors being bred in England. Nell was owned by the Earl of Home (1799–1881).

most important characteristics of the breed. In a letter of 1887, the third Earl of Malmesbury tells the sixth Duke of Buccleuch that "The real breed [Labrador Retriever] may be known by their having a close coat which turns the water off like oil and, above all, a tail like an otter." From the beginning, then, the practical value and sturdiness of the dog were very important. The Labrador Retriever had to be, and had to remain, a water- and weather-proof hunting dog.

The Duke of Buccleuch's Labradors

In 1911, Douglas Cairns wrote a lengthy article about the Labrador Retrievers of the Duke of Buccleuch at Langholm Lodge. In it we learn a great deal about the Labrador breed and the hunting practice and training of that time:

- Initially Labrador Retrievers were used mainly to bring back game shot over water. For retrieval on land, many other options existed, but for water retrieval and endurance, no other breed was their match.

- The growth in popularity of the Labrador, and the desire to control their breeding, is connected to the growth in popularity of grouse hunting. Labradors were trained to drive the birds and then, once shot, retrieve them from the water or swamps, as needed. Traditionally, the roles of driving and retrieving were separate, requiring different dogs for each purpose.

Figure 2.3 Avon, Nero, and Gyp, owned by the Duke of Buccleuch from Bowhill. Illustration from Arthur Wardle in *The Field* in the 1880s.

Figure 2.4 Avon, born in 1885, was bred by Lord Malmesbury and given to the Duke of Buccleuch.

Figure 2.5 A group of dogs from Langholm Lodge.

- Langholm Lodge developed a successful training style that began with a firm foundation of obedience before moving to nose work. Cairns notes how eager the dogs are to work each day and how they will not "run in" after game without first receiving a command.
- The key for the Langholm Lodge training method is that the dogs are trained, and used, to do what people cannot do. As Cairns points out, even an uneducated boy can see where game drops and collect it. But only a dog can find game using their nose. Restricting dogs to this specialty results in better dogs.

THE DUKE OF BUCCLEUCH'S LABRADORS AT LANGHOLM LODGE

by Douglas Cairns, in *Country Life*, December 2, 1911

It is a pity that no pictorial records are available to give us an idea of the Labrador dogs existing in England about 1840. Fresh blood was wanted, and obtained about that time, dogs being imported from Newfoundland by the Duke of Buccleuch, the Earl of Home and Lord John Scott, dogs very similar in type to those portrayed here, according to the testimony of some who remembered them. They were, however, larger, coarser and more dour; no doubt their hereditary treatment and surroundings would account for this latter trait. In common with other dogs used for sport at that time they were far more difficult to train than their descendants.

They excelled all other breeds in water, wherein, in those days, lay the retriever's chief occupation; game on land was killed under conditions which made its recovery less dependent on a retriever proper; the sportsman had his pointers, setters, or spaniels, mostly capable of retrieving if required to do so; probably the boy who carried the bag had powers of observation and eyesight unimpaired by so-called education; game was far less plentiful than now and sat closer; in fact, the difficulty lay more in flushing the bird than in recovering the corpse.

But in the early eighties of the 19th century, driving, or, at any rate, grouse-driving, had come to stay, and more retrievers were necessary. The Labrador in his purity had become scarce, though on most estates in the South of Scotland were to be found dogs containing a good deal of Labrador blood. At Langholm Lodge the retrievers were few in number and nondescript in appearance, and it was decided to establish in their stead a kennel from the strains considered then, as now, to be most suitable for the work required. Two dogs and a bitch from Lord Malmesbury, a bitch from Lord Ruthven, and an admixture of blood from the Duke of Hamilton's kennel formed the nucleus of the present race, which has occasionally been refreshed from the same blood established elsewhere.

The estate is one on which a large head of game is killed, particularly grouse, and in the retriever used for grouse-driving on a large scale endurance and nose are absolutely indispensable if the work of picking up is to be done with the celerity characteristic of Langholm methods. There are probably no moors where the collection is effected so quickly. This year there was a prodigious quantity of stuff to collect.

In addition to their nose, which is equalled in other breeds, and their endurance, which is not, a very noticeable feature in the work of these dogs is their speed; not merely the pace at which they cover the ground, but the lightning-like return and "delivery." This is the speed that really counts, not the headlong, brainless career, which takes a dog too fast for his nose and presently prostrates him panting in the heather.

There are other characteristics in the Langholm dogs which the intelligent critic will appreciate; for instance, a total absence of jealousy, each dog being more intent on using his own nose and doing his own job "on his own" than on tearing a bird from the jaws of his kennel companion. He will notice that each dog not only comes home with his tail up, after a strenuous day in any weather, but also is just as keen on Saturday as he was on Monday morning. He may be present when a couple of hundred hares are killed in a day partridge-shooting, but is unlikely to see a dog "run in." One or two old dogs are allowed to retrieve wounded hares when necessary; the rest are broken off fur entirely, and will "seek dead" for partridges with a total disregard for dead hares lying among them. After all, dead hares are best picked up by men, and total abstinence is desirable from every point of view, so far as dogs are concerned with "fur."

The Langholm dogs are educated almost entirely on driven grouse, often described as the very worst schooling a young dog can get. The truth of this sweeping statement depends upon circumstances and upon men. To hunt the canine pupil at complete liberty behind a line of butts, allowing him to range where he likes, is to turn him into a wild beast, with a supreme contempt for his tamer. To encourage him to gather birds lying in his view is also to court disaster, for we, too, have eyes; it is by his nose we wish him to assist us.

But, assuming that he is in the hands of a sensible man, from whom he has learnt obedience before ever being brought into action (a *sine qua non* in all sporting dogs), and also that he has "come in" with the drive, and not yet been promoted to a place of honour in a butt, it is another story all together. He will have seen many birds flushed, but when told to "seek dead" must do so without the incentive of having seen birds fall; must hunt by faith, and continue to do so, whether he finds much, little, or nothing to reward his perseverance.

True, this education is incomplete as a preparation for other forms of shooting. A retriever destined to work behind pointing dogs requires more finish; he is expected to drop when told, or signalled, and altogether to behave with more circumspection and gravity, but, given brains and a proper garden education in his puppyhood, he will soon learn to suit his behaviour to the occasion, and in the meanwhile has learnt to use his nose and to persevere.

The likeliest method of destroying a young retriever's chance of ever being useful for anything except marking is to hold him behind a line of guns and send him for birds as they fall in full view. The under-keeper (we trust the perpetrator of such mischief will never rise higher) thus saves himself some trouble and produces in a surprisingly short time a glaring, gallopping star-gazer, useless for finding anything but what can be gathered with less damage by a mere man.

The question used often to be and is still sometimes asked, "Are not Labradors apt to be hard-mouthed?" In the pure strain this fault is exceedingly rare, and when present can generally be traced to bad management. If the puppy is taught to bring an inanimate object, such as a glove, before being entered to game, which should be cold, or to peewits and curlews as a further preliminary step, it [the hard mouth] should be as extinct as the "dourness" of the breed referred to by Colonel Hawker.

Warm young grouse may possibly constitute a temptation, and in any case a dog is useless for the picking-up-the-next-day business unless he will find and carry cold game. The rapid return and "delivery," no less than the fine free temper so characteristic of the breed, lend neither time nor

Figure 2.6 *Portrait of Guy*, photographed by C. Reid.

Figure 2.7 Guy is the great-grandson of a dog bred by Lord Malmesbury in 1885.

encouragement to chewing, a habit probably more common in the pointer-retriever cross, sometimes described as "Labrador." The indications of this cross — the fine satin coat, thin skin, stinglike tail, peculiarly placed eye, prominent brisket — are conspicuously absent in the Langholm dogs. The true type of head and coat is clearly shown in Mr. Reid's head-and-neck

Figure 2.8 Captain was the favorite of the head gamekeeper at Langholm.

Figure 2.9 Bridget and Active, two veteran Labradors at Langholm Lodge (1911).

portrait of Guy, a great-grandson of a dog bred by Lord Malmesbury in 1885. Note the dense hair, wide, brainy skull and small Newfoundland-like ear. Active has placed many a season's hard work to her credit in a career now, alas! drawing near its close. Captain is the favourite of Smith, the head-keeper, to whom he is a fitting accompaniment. Greater praise no dog could win.

Criticism of the Breed

Despite the praise bestowed by Cairns, Labrador Retrievers were not uniformly admired at the end of the 19th and early 20th centuries. In 1881, the British cynologic author Vero Shaw was highly critical of the breed and its breeders:

> The term Retriever is in itself sufficiently indicative of the duties which this breed of dog is called upon to carry out, and these duties can, it is universally admitted, be successfully performed by many varieties besides the one in question. In fact, the very creation of the Retriever proper, as he now exists, is comparatively speaking of but recent date.
>
> In consequence probably of the recent introduction of the Retriever as a distinct variety into the dog family, there are numbers of very indifferent and unworthy specimens — to use a mild expression — of the breed to be found in all directions. These may, we think, reasonably be considered to be the results of some of the many experiments that no doubt have been made from time to time in breeding this sort of dog, which experiments in many cases have turned out disastrously for those whose fertile brains conceived the cross.
>
> At any rate, the almost countless number of black dogs which are seen in all parts of the country, and which are invariably styled Retrievers by those who are most interested in them, would cause it to be supposed that their owners, for the most part, are honestly under the belief that in doing so they are describing the animals correctly. It is not, however, only to sporting dogs alone that the art of retrieving game on

land or in water is confined, for many breeds of dogs which are by no means identified with sport in popular estimation can be taught to do so easily by any one with patience enough to undertake their education.[3]

By 1910, Henry James observed that the breed had become more uniform, although it was losing some important characteristics at the same time:

> Looking backwards some twenty five years or thereabouts in the history of the Labrador Dog, as it is known in this country, we cannot but recognise that an enormous improvement in type has been effected. And this improvement is all the more noticeable in that it is not due entirely, nor even chiefly, to shows, thereby differing from the development which takes place in one after another of the "fancy" breeds. That the improvement in Labrador type has been brought about with but very little sacrifice of efficiency will be readily admitted by anyone conversant with the performances in the breed, whether at Field Trials or in the ordinary conduct of a day's shooting, which often affords opportunities which cannot be stage-managed at the trials.
>
> [However,] one or two characteristics have been lost, or nearly lost, such as the big round "barrel," which, while denoting great space for heart and lungs, was usually slung between a pair of very indifferent shoulders; the dense undercoat also, rendering its wearer as waterproof as a seal, is passing, though we were glad to see, and feel, it on the winner at a recent Northern show where the class for the breed was headed by three excellent specimens. Without this coat no Labrador can be called perfect.
>
> The comparative rarity of that mental serenity, a quality difficult of definition but once a trait in the breed, probably a relic of the dourness resulting from countless generations' residence in a land of appalling climatic severity, is possibly due to the fact that Retrievers are now kept in greatly increased numbers, and thus see a good deal more of the inside of a kennel than of their masters' society.[4]

The Munden Labradors

A significant breakthrough for the Labrador Retriever took place in 1884 after Arthur Holland-Hibbert (later the third Viscount Knutsford) began his association with the breed. He founded Munden Kennel at Munden, near Watford, Hertfordshire, and was the first breeder to have his dogs registered in the stud books of the Kennel Club. He got his first Labrador from the Earl of Verulam: the female Munden Sybil, bred by Lord Grimston at Gorhambury, St. Albians, and tracing back to the famous dog Kielder, who descends from Netherby Boatswain, imported from Newfoundland by Sir Richard Graham, and Netherby Nell, whose origins are unknown. Viscount Knutsford characterized Munden Sybil as "a timid creature but a wonderfully good bitch for nose, pace, endurance and marking."[5]

Figure 2.10 Mr. Arthur Holland-Hibbert (Viscount Knutsford) with some of his dogs at Munden (1908).

The type of Labradors bred by Viscount Knutsford have many similarities to today's Labradors. For about 50 years, Munden Kennel has produced a succession of famous dogs whose blood runs like a thread through the whole fabric of the breed. A large proportion of these dogs trace back to Munden

ENGLISH BREEDING

Figure 2.11 The pick of Munden Kennel: (clockwise from the top) Sandfly, Sovereign, Saba, and Sorrow.

Sixty and Munden Scottie. About Munden Sixty, whelped in July 1897, Viscount Knutsford wrote in his breed-record book that "he was black with no white and a well-made dog" and later on, "to the everlasting grief of all who knew him, this splendid dog died August 1901."[6]

The Munden dogs were excellent workers and were often seen in field trials. Munden Single, born March 1899 as a daughter of Munden Sixty and Munden Scottie, was the first Labrador Retriever to run in a field trial. At that time, near the beginning of the 20th century, the best working dogs were Flat-Coated Retrievers, but such progress had been made in Labrador breeding that a substantial percentage of the prizes at retriever trials began to fall to Labradors. Munden Single was described as "exceeding good looking" and "the best game finder and steadiest retriever ever seen." Viscount Knutsford wrote of her death saying she "had to end her glorious life in September 1909. She now reposes in a glass case in the Natural History Museum, Kensington, as an example." However, he comments on the poor job of preserving her, saying "it is a bad representation" of such a marvelous dog.

In 1912, Douglas Cairns noted the exceptional contributions of Munden Kennel and Mr. Holland-Hibbert for the breed:

> Mr. Arthur Holland-Hibbert describes Munden Sapper as his best dog, now that Munden Sovereign is too old. His dam, Munden Sandfly, carries a head both wide and brainy. She is "slower than most of the kennel" and, therefore, probably a quick recoverer of game, as are many retrievers just slow enough not to waste time by over-running the scent.
>
> We give two portraits of Munden Sorrow, an own sister to Munden Saba but with five years in hand, and already, at two years old, her owner's best bitch. Munden Saba is an almost ideal brood bitch, although her portraits gives her a hollow back. No weediness here, but great bone, and almost a dog's [male's] head. She descends on her sire's side from Sir Richard Graham's celebrated Tar, while her dam, Munden Single (by Sixty out of Scottie) is three-quarters bred from the Duke of Buccleuch's kennel. Scottie's sire was Drake, born twenty-one

Figure 2.12 Munden Sapper (1911).

ENGLISH BREEDING

Figure 2.13 Munden Saba (1912).

Figure 2.14 Munden Shameful (1912).

years ago, than whom [sic] no better or wiser dog ever "wore hair."

Anxious to reproduce the lovely heads of Munden Single and her son, Munden Sovereign, Mr. Holland-Hibbert some time since took his courage in both hands and bred mother to son, and (here was salvation) the offspring to an outsider, comparatively speaking; result, Munden Shameful, a puppy whose beauty we trust will not tempt her owner to make any further experiments in the same risky direction. At any rate, the appearance of the litter argues well for the future, and betokens a degree of proper nourishment and care far in excess of that best owed upon the poor human mites whose lot these puppies may be destined indirectly to ameliorate. For to the Society for the Prevention of Cruelty to Children goes the price of every pup sold from the Munden kennel.[7]

ABBREVIATIONS OF BRITISH CHAMPIONSHIP TITLES

- CC   Challenge Certificate (Britain)
- Ch   Champion
- ShCh Show Champion
- FTCh Field Trial Champion

During World War I, the Labrador kennel at Munden became practically extinct, but after the war, Viscount Knutsford got a puppy from the Banchory kennel of Mrs. Lorna Dick (usually called Mrs. Quintin Dick and later Countess Howe in cynological records) to restart his breeding. This puppy, which he registered as Munden Scarcity (bred from Ch Banchory Lucky x Banchory Betty) was mated to Ch Banchory Bolo and produced Munden Solo. Later Viscount Knutsford owned Munden Squeezer, with which, at the age of 79, he won at two trials, handling the dog himself. At the Gamekeeper's Trials in 1935, Viscount Knutsford collapsed when speaking as Chairman of the Labrador Club at the luncheon and died.

Kennel Club Recognition

In 1903, the Kennel Club in England recognized the Labrador Retriever as a breed. Only black Labrador Retrievers were accepted at shows, although there were already yellows and chocolates. For instance, it is known that in 1892 two "liver colored" Labrador pups were born at Buccleuch's kennel, and in 1899, the first yellow Labrador Retriever on record, Ben of Hyde, was born at the kennel of Major C. J. Radclyffe. Probably this refusal of other colors was because hunters preferred the black Labs and breeders catered to their preference.

Flapper

Major Portal's dog Flapper was, in 1907 and 1908, the first Labrador Retriever to win the Field Trial Champion title. He was born in 1902 from the Malmesbury Sweep and Buccleuch lines, and he delighted all who saw him at work. He also left a very numerous and illustrious progeny: 700 puppies and over 30 field trial winners!

Figure 2.15 Flapper, the first Labrador to win the Field Trial Champion title.

Ch Brayton Swift was another cornerstone upon which the breed was securely built, a vital sire that was used with tremendous effect by the Whitmore kennel of Major Twyford.

Peter of Faskally

With such exceptional performers, the imagination of the public was roused, but interest in the breed rose to great intensity when Captain A. E. Butter brought out Peter of Faskally and demonstrated a method of training and handling that left nothing to chance.

Peter of Faskally was bred by Mr. Watson of Birkhill and was born in 1908 from a mating between Waterdale Gamester and Birkhill Juliet. He was three generations in direct male line to Munden Sixty and Munden Scottie.

Faskally Estate, near Pitlochry, Scotland, had been the seat of the Butter family from its purchase in 1778 by Mr. Henry Butter. The Labrador Retrievers on the estate were the property of Mr. Archibald Edward Butter and his wife Helen Cicely Kerr (whose name in historical records is recorded as Mrs. Archibald

Figure 2.16 Peter of Faskally brings a pheasant to Captain A. E. Butter.

ENGLISH BREEDING

Figure 2.17 Peter of Faskally in 1911. Peter of Faskally is an ancestor for all present-day chocolate Labradors.

Figure 2.18 Captain and Mrs. Butter (with, on the left, the still young Peter of Faskally and, on the right, Dungavel Juno at about one year old (1908).

Butter). As well as a keen sportsman and big-game hunter who traveled all over the world, Captain Butter was also an adept gun dog trainer. Mrs. Butter, too, was exceptionally skilled and was one of the first women to compete against men in Kennel Club trials. The couple owned and trained a series of Labrador Retrievers whose prefix, Faskally, appeared consistently on gun dog trial leader-boards in the decade running up to World War I.

A NEW TRAINING METHOD

The Butters' training techniques were new for the time and were based on methods used to train sheepdogs. Until this point, dogs were trained for field trials using the "dog-breaking" method. This involved allowing dogs to make mistakes and then punishing them harshly so they wouldn't make the mistake again.

The Butters instead used an intensive training system using rewards, whistle signals, and gestures. Through this training, the Butters' dogs worked faster and more efficiently and had perfect results at field trials. The Butters' method required dogs of exceptional intelligence that would obey the slightest signal of the handler. The team of Captain Butter and Peter of Faskally, in perfect teamwork, won stake after stake, including the field trial championship of 1911.

Not even a registered breed for field trials in the last decade of the 19th century, the Labrador made a spectacular entry into the sporting scene in the first decade of the 20th century. In the last full season before World War I, 179 of the 247 dogs entered for the fourteenth field trials in Britain were Labradors. This surge can be attributed largely to the Duke of Buccleuch's Labradors, which, although they never campaigned in field trial competitions, became the basis of the good blood in many Labrador field trial champions in the early 20th century:

- 1904: Arthur Holland-Hibbert's Labrador, Munden Single, which was almost pure Buccleuch and Malmesbury blood, was the first of the breed to take a card at a field trial.
- 1906: Major Maurice Mortal's FTCh Flapper, also of Buccleuch blood, was the first to be placed.

- 1910: Peter of Faskally, who had much Buccleuch blood on both sides, became the only retriever to win two open stakes in one season.
- 1911: Peter of Faskally is the first field trial champion to compete in an entry composed entirely of Labradors.

About Peter of Faskally's field trial in Scotland in October 1910, the *Dundee Courier* observed the following:

> Alert, silent and with a carriage graceful for a retriever, Peter goes about his work in thorough earnest, and once on the trail of either feather or fur, he locates his quarry speedily, and returns with his spoil in his mouth, scarcely showing teeth marks at all.[8]

Seen in Figure 2.19, Mrs. Butter's bitch Dungavel Jet was bred in April 1907 by the Duchess of Hamilton from Mr. Portal's Flapper with Dungavel Juno and bought by the Butters in 1911. Like her mate, Peter of Faskally, Jet was well admired in the field

Figure 2.19 *Portrait of the black Labrador "Peter of Faskally" holding a cock pheasant, with his mate "Dungavel Jet" in a landscape*, a 1912 painting by Maud Earl. Stud records show that Peter and Jet produced numerous litters.

trials of 1910 and 1911. She won the Kennel Club's All-Age Stake at Lord Lonsdale's Estate at Lowther, Westmoreland, after which *The Field* magazine commented the following: "Butter then put Dungavel Jet on the line, and the bitch quickly got her nose down and brought the hare smartly to hand."[9]

The Butters owned a second estate at Balmer Hall, Little Snoring, near Fakenham, West Norfolk, and the end-of-season championship of 1911 was held there. Just before the event, a commentator from *The Field* noted the equality between Peter and Jet: "The running of the Balmer Hall brace, Mrs. Butter's Dungavel Jet and Peter of Faskally, property of Mr. Butter, will be followed with interest for it is recognised that either Lab might win."[10]

In 1912, the *Kennel Gazette* could hardly control its rapture over Peter:

> I have no hesitation in describing Mr. A. E. Butter's Peter of Faskally as the most notable performer of the year … Peter to my mind combines to perfection all the qualities that are claimed for Labradors, great speed, sagacity, excellent nose, and absolutely tender mouth, and while spendidly endowed with initiative, he is not above taking a hint from his master.

Major Maurice Portal, owner of FTCh Flapper, would later write the following:

> That the Labrador was not more generally popular in the 1904 days is strange. True, until 1903 the Kennel Club did not recognize the breed, but in about 1837 the Earl of Malmesbury of that day had a kennel which was at its maximum about 1870, while Sir Richard Graham had a kennel at Netherby in 1860. The Duke of Buccleuch and the Hon. A. Holland-Hibbert also had large kennels in the 1880–84 days, and there were other owners. The breed seems to date its popularity from the days of Peter of Faskally, handled by the incomparable handler, the late Captain A. E. Butter. The writer's Flapper was also one of the pioneers, his great sagacity and game-finding ability helping to bring credit to the breed. These two dogs were used extensively at stud

and are responsible for a very large percentage of the field trial Labradors of today.[11]

That Peter passed on his excellent working drive and perfect character will be clear from the results of his progeny: 32 of them won a prize at field trials. And there was more: Peter of Faskally was the sire of FTCh Patron of Faskally, who also won the Champion Stake in 1913, as did Patron's son, Tag of Whitmore, in 1920, thus setting a record for three generations winning the important Champion Stake trophy. Mr. Twyford considered his Tag "one of the best, if not the best field trial dog ever," bred and owned by his Whitmore kennel.

The Banchory Retrievers

Mrs. Lorna Dick (after her second marriage, in 1927, Countess Howe) was also an important figure in Labrador Retriever breed history. In 1912, she encountered the breed for the first time, and her first Labrador was Scandal of Glynn, a son of Peter of Faskally. Because of his engaging character, the Lab stole Mrs. Dick's heart. In 1914, she started a kennel, and supported by her kennel manager, Mr. T. Gaunt, Banchory Kennel became one of the most important dual-purpose kennels in England (specializing in dogs that are both show and field trial champions).

Mrs. Dick was distressed at the loss of her beloved Scandal of Glynn at the age of five in 1917, and with great difficulty, she traced his only son, Banchory Bolo. Bolo was born in December 1915 in the only litter Scandal had. Here is her account of Bolo's amazing story:

> He had been through various hands, and various trainers had tried to train him. He was offered to me with the proviso that if I could not make anything of him I was to have him destroyed. In fact he had what human beings would describe as a really bad police record. However, I accepted him gratefully.
>
> It was arranged that I should meet him at Liverpool Station, so one February morning in 1918, I went there

to greet him and found a disconsolate, surly dog, heavily muzzled. I took him to the house we had in Grosvenor Crescent and left him off his chain in my bedroom. It took me nearly an hour to catch him, so terrified was he. He must have got a chill on the journey — it was bitterly cold. He was ill for nearly three weeks. During those weeks he gained confidence in me and could hardly bear me out of his sight. When he got well, I took him with me to Scotland and started to train him to be steady to the gun. This I did by at first shooting rabbits with a rifle out of a pony cart. He gradually learnt not to run-in and eventually became one of the steadiest dogs I have ever known.

We then moved down to the place we had in Shropshire and I got Bolo ready to run in field trials. Unfortunately he went with me one evening to the stable yard where he heard one of the stable boys cracking a whip. The old terror came back to him and he bolted. Finally at midnight I gave up searching for him and went to my room, leaving the front door open. At 5 a.m. Bolo came into my room and got into his basket. When I was about to go to my bath an hour later I was horrified to see big splashes of blood on the floor. On examining Bolo I found he had two very deep wounds on his chest, a tear three inches long in his groin, and his hind leg and hock torn so badly that the bone was visible. I was urged to have him destroyed but this I would not do. The nearest veterinary surgeon lived eight miles away; there was no telephone and I knew he would be away at a market town another eight miles away; so with the kennel man I had then, I put twenty-three stitches into Bolo. He was so good and lay perfectly still until all was finished. Of course there could be no question of competing at field trials that season.

The following season he became a field trial champion, winning the Open Stake at the Western Counties Field Trial Meeting and the Scottish Open Stakes in quick succession. He soon qualified as a show champion, thus becoming the first dual champion Labrador. It was as a sire that Bolo proved of such enormous value. As he was always with me he was not heavily used as a stud dog, but I think every litter sired by

Figure 2.20 Banchory Bolo, the first dual champion Labrador Retriever.

him contained a winner at trials and on the show bench. Most of the Labradors winning at trials and at shows today are descended from him.[12]

And indeed, Banchory Bolo, the first dual champion, sired more champions than any other Labrador Retriever before him. In the ranks of the field trial winners of that time, two out of three are descendants of Bolo.

One of the greatest celebrities from Banchory Kennel was Ch Ilderton Ben, whose value did not diminish with the years. He was notable as the sire of the second Labrador dual champion, Banchory Sunspeck, also owned by Mrs. Dick. In 1916, Mrs. Dick was the first secretary of the Labrador Retriever Club. She encouraged game wardens to work with Labrador Retrievers and took care of classes for Labrador Retrievers at the famous Crufts Dog Show. The number of both Labradors and Labrador enthusiasts increased through her efforts.

World War I

After World War I, Labrador Retrievers surpassed Flat-Coated Retrievers in popularity. The latter were mostly in the possession of gamekeepers, who did their military service during the

Figure 2.21 A number of Labradors with their handlers at the Labrador Retriever Club's 25th field trial competition in 1935.

war and couldn't afford to keep their kennels afterward. The Labrador Retriever, however, was mostly in the hands of the nobility, who even during difficult times were able to keep their kennels and breeding programs operating. Moreover, a number of high-class Labradors had been purchased from England by

Figure 2.22 Banchory Kennel was famous worldwide. Countess Howe's excellent Labradors were as successful in the show rings as they were in field trials.

breeders in the United States who recognized the merits of the breed. Previously, the sporting princes of India had been the chief buyers in the British market, while a few other dogs had gone each year to China and various British colonies. Now the United States became an important market for English breeders.

Other Dual Champions

Many gamekeepers found the Labrador Retriever easier to train than the Flat-Coated Retriever and its short coat an advantage

Figure 2.23 Countess Howe with three noted champions from her kennel: Bramshaw Bob, Ingleston Ben, and Banchory Trueman.

Figure 2.24 Bramshaw Bob won six field trial honors and 10 Challenge Certificates. He became champion in 1932 and became a dual champion in 1933.

when working in water. Because there were as many as seven Labrador dual champions in the time between the world wars, the future of the breed was assured. These holders of the Dual Champion title will always command a measure of attention in the history of the Labrador.

Dual Champion Titus of Whitmore, bred and owned by Mr. T. W. Twyford, won the Champion Stake in 1923, and his 1922-born son, Flute of Flodden, bred by Lord Joicey, also became a dual champion.

Given the reputation of her kennel, it is not surprising that Countess Howe (formerly Mrs. Dick) would own several dual champion dogs. The fifth dual champion in the breed was Bramshaw Bob; he was purchased by the Countess from Sir George Thursby in December 1931. He was very much in the public eye, having won Best in Show at the Crufts Dog Show for two years in succession (1932 and 1933). His sire, Ch Ingleston Ben, also owned by the Countess, was runner-up in Labradors at Crufts in 1932. Ingleston Ben's other son, Ch Cheverells Ben of Banchory, was Best in Show at Crufts in 1938. Finally, Banchory

Painter, born in 1930, was also a dual champion, as was the 1933-born bitch Lochar Nessie, bred by Mr. T. Dinwoodie and owned by Mr. Morris.

Post-1945

Toward the end of the 1930s, and even more after World War II, it became clear that not every breeder was looking for dual purpose Labrador Retrievers. Not everyone wanted to hunt or train the dogs for hunting, which was a lot more work than preparing the dogs for show. A big difference in appearance developed between the Labrador Retrievers registered for shows and those working in field trials. Fortunately, later breeders once again bred more purposefully towards a uniformity in type. But in spite of this, the difference between show and working Labrador Retrievers continued to exist and only a few Labrador Retrievers obtained the Dual Champion title.

Among the first dual champions after World War II were the following:
- the black Labrador Staindrop Saighdear, born in 1944 and owned by Mr. Edgar Winter
- the black Labrador Rockstead Footspark, born in 1945 and owned by Mr. R. MacDonald
- the yellow Labrador Knaith Banjo, born in 1946 and bred and owned by Mrs. Veronica Wormald

The Sandylands Retrievers

In this historic overview of the Labrador breed, Gwen Broadley's famous Sandylands Kennel has to be mentioned. Worldwide, Gwen Broadley enjoyed great fame because of the excellent character and top-notch quality of her dogs. About selecting a suitable stud dog, she wrote, "Never forget that a good character and health, both genetic, are two important things to watch, because without those a dog is worthless."[13]

Broadley's first dog, a pet Labrador, was born in 1929 and registered as Juno of Sandylands. Someone told her Juno was worth showing, and at his first show he won two first prizes. That was the start of her kennel and the prefix "Sandylands"

Figure 2.25 Pictured here are four Sandylands champions from the 1950s: (left to right) Beau, Belle, Jilly, and Justice. The fifth dog is Ch British Justice of Banchory Kennel.

Figure 2.26 Ch Sandylands Truth, born in 1960.

was registered with the Kennel Club in 1931. After that, Broadley bought a black Labrador and registered him as Jerry of Sandylands. He became the first Sandylands champion, the first of many big winners from her kennel, and he and Juno are behind the top Sandylands winners of the present day. Of Sandylands Kennel's success, Richard Edwards writes:

> Only Countess Howe's Banchory Kennel can claim the same sort of fame in Labradors that Sandylands enjoys, but Countess Howe brought in most of her top show winners, whereas many of the Sandylands champions are homebred. Over the years Gwen brought in stock, but always there was this bloodline back to the originals, Jerry and Juno. In this sense there is continuity to the Sandylands Labradors and it runs on to the present day.[14]

In the immediate postwar period, a number of Labrador Retrievers from Sandylands were exported to the United States: in particular, the yellow male Ch Landyke Patrick and the big-winning black bitch Ch Sandylands Harley Princess. Before she was exported, Harley Princess had a litter that included Ch Sandylands Belle of Helenspring, who had been sold but was bought back to Sandylands to replace her mother. Belle was to prove a brilliant dam. In three litters to Ch British Justice, Belle produced Ch Sandylands Justice, Ch Sandylands Jilly, and ShCh Sandylands Juno. In a later litter to Ch Whatstandwell Coronet, Belle was the dam of the lovely black Ch Sandylands Cora.

In his 1949 review of Sandylands Kennel, Mr. Frank Warner Hill wrote the following:

> Arriving at the top in any sphere is a long and arduous experience, and once established, remaining there is doubly difficult. Thus we appreciate the continued high standing of Mrs. Gwen Broadley's gun dog kennel which houses five Labrador champions, two of which have been added this year. The champions are Ch Landyke Patrick, Ch June of Sandylands, Ch Sandylands Blackberry, Ch Sandylands Harley Superb and Ch Sandylands Beau.[15]

For two years in the mid-1950s, Gwen Broadley joined forces with Countess Howe to form Banchory-Sandylands. However, after a serious accident, the countess was forced to give up her dogs, so Broadley set up Sandylands Kennel at Lower

Shuckburgh. There she bred her champion dogs for the next 40 years. Richard Edwards comments on this period:

> Around this time, the late 1950s, the Sandylands Kennel needed a stud dog, and Gwen asked for a puppy from a litter bred by Mr. and Mrs. G. Cairns, and so the legendary Ch Sandylands Tweed of Blaircourt arrived at Sandylands. Tweed proved to be a critically important influence upon the show Labrador and he added a new level of authority to an already extremely important kennel. Tweed's grandson, Tandy, was the first major yellow stud dog at Sandylands.
>
> As the show Labrador scene expanded with new prosperity in Britain in the 1960s, the Sandylands prefix became more and more central to the breed. After a slow start to his stud career, … the black Ch Sandylands Mark (1965), a son of the lovely Ch Sandylands Truth … produced champion after champion for so many grateful breeders. Having purchased the lovely ShCh Sandylands Star of Jayncourt from Gwen previously, in the early 1970s, Mr. Garner Anthony of Hawaii became a partner with Gwen in the Sandylands prefix and kennel.[16]

The 1970s proved to be another golden era of winning for the kennel. A whole string of top-winning Labradors were taken to their British championship from Sandylands itself. Across the 1980s and 1990s, Gwen Broadley and Garner Anthony continued to produce top-winning Labradors. Ch Sandylands My Guy was a great ambassador for the breed, with his lovely quiet style, and in ShCh Sandylands Bliss, the kennel had one of the very best show Labradors of any era. Bliss died whelping the litter that included ShCh Sandylands Gad-About, who was a successful sire with some lovely top-winning yellow pups.

Erica Jayes started working at Sandylands as a child helping in the kennels. However, over the years, she took on more responsibility, and when Broadley died at the age of 92 in 1999, Jayes took over the Sandylands prefix and worked in partnership with Garner Anthony and his wife, Barbara.[17]

Up to April 2007, there had been over 85 Sandylands British champions, one of the last being ShCh Sandylands Wait Awhile.

Author David Craig tried to register the number of foreign Sandylands champions but stopped after he found over 100.[18] Since Barbara Anthony's death in 2011, the kennel and the Sandylands prefix have been in the sole name of Erica Jayes, and the kennel has relocated to Greystones, near Ufton, in the vicinity of Leamington Spa, just 6 miles (9.7 km) from the old Sandylands at Lower Shuckburgh.

FAMOUS LABRADOR OWNERS

The British royal family have long appreciated Labrador Retrievers, and the royal family's interest in breeding, showing, and training Labs helped make the breed wildly popular in England and abroad as a pet and gun dog. King George V (1865–1936) loved the breed and exhibited Labrador Retrievers at several of the leading shows. The royal kennels now use the Sandringham prefix but had previously used Wolverton, which produced quite a few noted winners. The Sandringham Labradors of Queen Elizabeth were also very successful in field trials, accompanied by their trainer Mr. W. Meldrum. The Queen's Labradors are still bred and kept in Sandringham Kennel. All the puppies born at Sandringham are named by the Queen herself and are registered at the Kennel Club.

The royal kennels date back to 1879, when King Edward VII (1841–1910) built kennels on the southern boundary of the grounds of Sandringham House. His wife, Queen Alexandra, owned many dog breeds, including the Sandringham strain of black Labradors, founded in 1911. Within the grounds of Sandringham is a burial ground for some of the much-loved dogs of previous monarchs. Today's kennels house about 20 dogs, including Labradors and Springer and Cocker Spaniels.

Among the Dutch royal family, Princess (previously Queen) Beatrix and her son King Willem-Alexander have Labrador Retrievers for hunting and very occasionally breeding.

Other royals with Labradors include Prince Juan Carlos from Spain, who got a black Labrador Retriever in 1962, and King Carl Gustav and his wife, Queen Silvia of Sweden, got a yellow Labrador Retriever in 2004.

Other prominent individuals also like Labs as pets. Bill Clinton, the 42nd president of the United States, had a chocolate Labrador, Buddy, from 1997 to 2002. According to a police report, Buddy was killed by a car while "playfully chasing a contractor" who had left the Clinton home in Chappaqua, New York. Secret Service agents rushed Buddy to an animal hospital, where he

Figure 2.27 Prince Albert (later King George VI) and his wife Elizabeth Bowes-Lyon, with their yellow Labrador (1920s). The dark butterscotch shade of yellow was typical of that time.

Figure 2.28 The king's Labradors at the Crufts Dog Show, 1932.

ENGLISH BREEDING

Figure 2.29 Queen Elizabeth II with her Labrador Retrievers at Balmoral in 1971.

Figure 2.30 The Dutch King Willem-Alexander with his Labrador Retrievers Skipper (right) and Nala in 2017.

Figure 2.31 Bill Clinton, former president of the United States, with Buddy, his chocolate Labrador, in 1999.

was pronounced dead. Some months later, Clinton acquired Seamus, another chocolate Labrador Retriever and Buddy's great nephew.[19]

Yellow Labradors

Among hunters, black was always the favorite color for the breed. But yellow Labradors have been in litters from the beginning, even though many breeders either killed or gave away yellow puppies because hunters were not interested in them. An 1850 oil painting shows Mrs. Joséphine Bowes sitting at a table with her yellow Labrador Bernardine lying at her feet. In the same museum is another painting by the same artist showing Bernardine lying on straw in front of a wall.

Figure 2.34 shows one of the earliest depictions of a yellow Retriever working. The painting shows a group of nobles, including William Lamb, the prime minister of England at the time, on a shooting estate. Scottie Westfall discusses the dogs:

> In this painting are two retrievers in attendance. One lying down is a black and tan dog that clearly resembles a dog of

Figure 2.32 *Joséphine Bowes, Countess of Montalbo,* by Antoine Dury.

the collie type. The other is an obvious yellow dog retrieving a pheasant cock. He is somewhat like a yellow Labrador, but the coat is more profuse and perhaps even lightly feathered. Here was a yellow retriever, not quite a golden or a wavy coat, working as a gun dog for the Whig gentry. It is an interesting painting, for it gives us an idea of the diversity that once was the retriever dog. If it could retrieve, it was a retriever, and it was bred to other dogs that retrieved. That's why so many different dogs were used to found the retriever breeds. And why they varied so much in appearance.[20]

Figure 2.33 *Bernardine (Mrs. Bowes's Dog)*, by Antoine Dury.

Figure 2.34 *The Shooting Party – Ranton Abbey*, by Francis Grant, 1840.

In 1899, out of two black parents, the yellow Labrador Ben of Hyde was born at the kennel of Major C. J. Radclyffe. This dog was intensively used by fanciers of the yellow color, and he proved to be a good sire for yellow Labrador Retrievers. Gradually the yellow Labradors received broader interest.

Figure 2.35 The yellow Labrador Ben of Hyde (born 1899) lying beside his daughter Dinah (born 1905).

Two enthusiastic supporters of the yellow Labradors were Lord Lonsdale and Mrs. Veronica Wormald, who with her Knaith Kennel had a lot of success. Yet the yellow dogs remained relatively rare. The first time Mrs. Wormald showed a yellow Labrador at Crufts Dog Show in London, she of course entered the ring for Labrador Retrievers. When the ring steward pointed out that the Golden Retrievers were shown in another ring, Mrs. Wormald remained firm, refused to leave, and won a prize with her yellow Labrador.

YELLOW LABRADOR RETRIEVER CLUB
In order to gain more recognition, the Yellow Labrador Retriever Club was founded in 1925. At first yellow Labradors had a different breed standard from the black ones. The most important difference was that "the neck must be thick and may show dewlap, and the tail may be carried curled over the back" on the yellow variety. After a few years, this breed standard was changed to match the breed standard of the black variety.

Figure 2.36 The first yellow Labrador dual champion Knaith Banjo, born in 1946 and bred and owned by Mrs. Veronica Wormald.

Yellow Labrador Retrievers grew in popularity, and by 1946, two of the three dual champions were yellow. Partly through the great effort of Mrs. Wormald, who was still showing her dogs at Crufts in 1978 at the age of 94, yellow Labrador Retrievers became as popular as the black ones. A few years ago, interest in the yellow Labs was pushed aside by the chocolates, but nowadays the yellow has again regained top interest.

Chocolate Labradors

About the early origin of the liver-colored or chocolate Labrador Retriever, less is known. Later in the breed history, we know that in 1892, two liver-colored Labrador pups were born at Buccleuch Kennel. Buccleuch Avon is said to have sired liver-colored pups and is considered the ancestor of the American field champion chocolate line.

We also know that in 1938, Dr. Montgomery bred a litter that included two chocolates, but what became of them is not recorded. It's a pity that there was less interest for this type, because very nice Labrador Retrievers can be bred of this rather rare color. Well-known chocolate Labs include Tibshelfs Bronze

(1954), Tibshelfs Choc (1964), and Tibshelfs Chocolate Simba (1972).

Mrs. Pauling of Cookridge Kennel showed the chocolate type's merit with her dog Cookridge Tango, the first chocolate Labrador Retriever that, in tight competition with black and yellow Labs, took the title of champion in 1964. In 1977, Lawnwoods Hot Chocolate became the first chocolate dog to win the show championship; after that, Lawnwoods Hot Chocolate also became US champion. Another well-known chocolate dog was the 1969-born International Show Champion and Field Trial Champion Puhs Atos.

During the mid-1980s, the chocolates garnered more interest, and for this increase the chocolate dog Wetherlam Nutcracker and the black Balnova Sultan were key sires, along with dogs from Donalbain and Kampsall kennels. However, the enormous expansion of the chocolate Labrador in recent years has left its marks on the breed due to narrow inbreeding to get the desired color in spite of health risks for the dogs.

Black Labrador Retrievers that carry the chocolate gene nowadays are in the majority, and in 1999, one in three Labrador puppies born in the United Kingdom were chocolates. Serious

Figure 2.37 Champion chocolate Labrador, Cookridge Tango (1964).

Figure 2.38 ShCh 1977 and American Ch Lawnwoods Hot Chocolate.

British breeders are sure that this color became popular through the influence of puppy farms and rapid breeding to get chocolate Labs.

Although now and then chocolates win their classes, usually black and yellow Labradors dominate British dog shows. And although the number of chocolates in the fields have increased, black Labs still dominate in competitions.

Labradors in the United States

In the early 20th century in the United States, the Scottish style of shooting became popular, and as a status symbol, people imported Scottish gamekeepers. Importation of these gamekeepers in turn led to the importation of Labrador Retrievers. The first Labrador registered in the American Kennel Club (AKC) stud book was the Scottish bitch Brocklehirst Floss in 1917, the year that the AKC recognized the breed. But the AKC still classified Labradors with the blanket term "retrievers," and it was not until the late 1920s that the retrievers were split up into the breeds we know today (discussed on pages ix–xiv). In 1927, there were only 23 Labradors registered, and it wasn't until after the article "Meet the Labrador Retriever" appeared in the *American Kennel Gazette* in July 1928 that the breed became more well known.

Figure 2.39 *American Kennel Gazette,* 1928.

After the 1930s, the breed gained popularity, and there was a great influx of British dogs into North America. Pioneers of the breed in America were Mr. J. F. Carlisle, Mr. F. B. Lord, Mr. and Mrs. Ferguson, and Mrs. Milbank and her husband, Dr. Samuel Milbank, the president of the Labrador Retriever Club of America, which was formed in 1931. In that year, the club also held the first American field trial for Labrador Retrievers at the Glenmere Court Estate in Chester, New York.

In 1929, the dog Kinclaven Lowesby was the first yellow Labrador Retriever registered in the AKC stud book. He was an imported son of FTCh Hayler's Defender and registered as the color "golden." In 1932, Diver of Chiltonfoliat was the first "liver colored" Labrador Retriever registered by the AKC. He was heavily line bred with Borris de Main, a yellow bitch born in 1920, who was said to carry the chocolate gene. But as both parents and all four grandparents of Diver were yellows, this dog could have been a very dark yellow rather than a true chocolate.

Mr. F. B. (Frank) Lord was a close friend of Countess Howe, and he acquired many dogs from her famous kennel. Banchory Kennel therefore figured prominently in the Labrador's start in the United States. One of these dogs was Banchory Trace, whose son Boli of Blake became the first American Labrador Retriever champion on November 1, 1933.

But Frank Lord wasn't the only one to acquire stock from the famous Banchory Kennel. Early enthusiasts of the breed, Mr. W. Averill Harriman of Arden Kennel, as well as Mr. J. F. Carlisle, became the cornerstones of the breed's beginnings in the United States.

On May 18, 1933, the first American annual specialty show for Labrador Retrievers was held in New York City and judged by Mrs. Marshall Field. Best in Show was awarded to Boli of Blake, owned by Mr. F. B. Lord. Another famous Best in Show Labrador of that time was Ch Earlsmoor Moor of Arden, who belonged to Mrs. and Dr. Samuel Milbank. Earlsmoor Moor of Arden also ran and placed in field trials. Although Labradors were a relatively rare breed in that time, Earlsmoore Moor of Arden's show records would, even today, be considered remarkable:

- Shown: 42 times
- Best of breed: 40 times
- Placed in sporting group: 27 times
- Won sporting group: 12 times
- Awarded Best in Show: 5 times
- Won the national specialty: 5 times

In 1938, the first picture of a dog appeared on the cover of *Life* magazine. It was the black Labrador Retriever Blind of Arden owned by Mr. W. Averell Harriman. At four years of age, Blind won the top US Retriever stake in November that year. The first clearly American-bred chocolate Labrador, Kennoway's

Fudge, was registered in the AKC stud book in 1940. This dog was line bred from the English dog FTCh Banchory Night Light, who descended from Buccleuch Avon. In 1941, the National Retriever Club was established in the United States.

The two world wars greatly diminished the breed's numbers (as it did the numbers of other breeds), but the social and economic changes that developed after World War II led to growing popularity of Labradors throughout the United States. The famous Sandylands Kennel especially influenced the shape and direction the show lines took in America through imports going back to Ch Sandylands Mark. Another influential dog, especially in field trial lines, includes American Dual Champion Shed of Arden, a grandson of Dual Champion Banchory Bolo. And the first dog ever to appear on a US stamp was the famous black Labrador King Buck, in 1959.

The 1991-born Storm's Riptide Star became the first chocolate Labrador to earn the American National Field Champion title with his win in 1996. His pedigree extends back to Buccleuch Avon, born in 1885.

Figure 2.40 The stamp by artist Maynard Reece, featuring King Buck of Nilo Kennels.

3

The Breed Standard

To say a dog is *purebred* means the animal meets the breed standard, a formal description of the ideal characteristics, temperament, and appearance of a breed. The breed standard for the Labrador Retriever was established at the beginning of the 20th century.

Thanks to the breed standard, all dogs within a breed are very similar, not only in appearance, but also in character and behavior. When interpreting the breed standard, always keep in mind that the Labrador is a hunting dog. The key words in the breed description are that it is "strong built and wide both in terms of body and head, agile and very active, friendly, willing and intelligent." So here we see a combination of physical and mental qualities. The Labrador's physique ensures that it can perform its duties well, and its character traits ensure it is a valued working dog and a pleasant companion.

The breed standards of the Labrador Retriever in different countries and organizations show considerable agreement (leading, at least in theory, to some degree of international uniformity). The various breed standards also stipulate requirements that are, in the main, not merely aesthetically desirable, but also have some justification in terms of producing a sound, intelligent working dog.

In this chapter we take a look at the Labrador breed standards of the American Kennel Club (AKC), the Canadian

THE BREED STANDARD

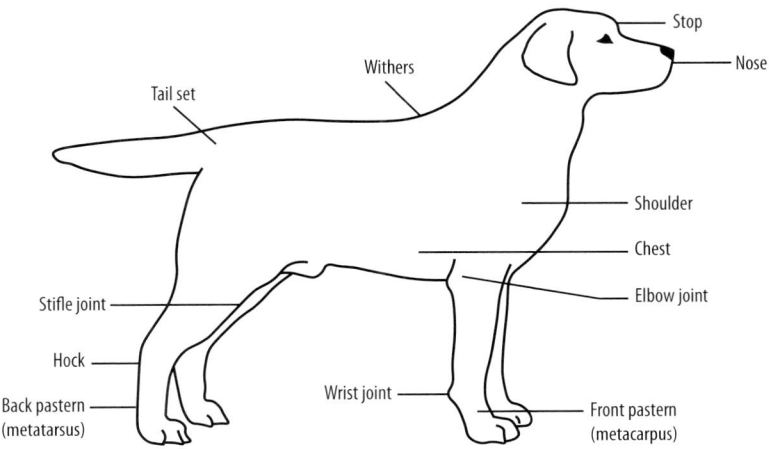

Figure 3.1 Points of the Labrador Retriever.

Kennel Club (CKC), the Kennel Club of Great Britain (KC), the Fédération Cynologique Internationale (FCI), and the United Kennel Club (UKC).[1]

A breed standard includes a lot of information, but many statements are open to different interpretations. How big are "medium-sized eyes" and "not large ears"? When are the shoulders "well placed"? What does one mean by "a tail of medium length"? In this chapter, we will discuss various points in an effort to interpret the intending meaning of the words.

Origin and Purpose

BREED STANDARD

The Labrador Retriever originated and developed on the island of Newfoundland as an all-purpose water dog, where fishermen were seen to use a dog of similar appearance to retrieve fish. An excellent water dog, his weather-resistant coat and unique tail, likened to that of an otter because of its shape, emphasize this trait.

The breed was preserved in England after anti-dog legislation almost decimated the breed in its homeland. Comparatively speaking, the Labrador is not a very old breed, its breed club having been formed in 1916 and the Yellow Labrador Club having been founded in 1925.

The Labrador Retriever is noted for its love of retrieving and water, for its excellent nose, soft mouth, intelligence, and biddable temperament. Extraordinary versatility allows Labradors to excel as hunting, service, and therapy dogs; in search and rescues; in drug and bomb detection; as family companions; and in performance and field events.

General Appearance

BREED STANDARD

Medium sized, strongly built, compact, short-coupled, very active (which precludes excessive body weight or substance); broad in skull; broad and deep through chest and ribs; broad and strong over loins and hindquarters. A water-resistant double coat, otter tail, and sound temperament are essential breed characteristics.

The starting point in the breed standard is a dog that is fit for function with absolute soundness, not exaggerated in any part. The general impression that a Labrador Retriever should give is that of a strong, broad, powerful dog, and this because of its wide, deep chest and ribs, and its well-developed muscles. This *does not* include a broad back and loins thanks to an excessive layer of fat!

The AKC standard emphasizes this in a separate point: "Substance and bone proportionate to the overall dog. Light, 'weedy' individuals are definitely incorrect; equally objectionable are cloddy lumbering specimens. Labrador Retrievers shall be shown in working condition, well-muscled and without excess fat."

Proportions and Size

BREED STANDARD

Proportions: Short coupled. Distance from withers to elbow approximately equal to distance from elbow to ground; length from point of shoulder to point of rump very slightly longer than height at withers. The brisket should extend to the elbows, but not perceptibly deeper. The body must be of sufficient length to permit a straight, free, and efficient stride, but the dog should never appear low and long or tall and leggy. A well-balanced dog is the ideal.

Size:

AKC, CKC, and UKC Sizes

	MALES	FEMALES
Height at the withers	22.5–24.5 in. (57–62 cm)	21.4–23.5 in. (54–60 cm)
Weight	60–80 lb. (27.27–36.36 kg)	55–75 lb. (25–34.09 kg)

The size standard of the KC and the FCI have one difference:

	MALES	FEMALES
Height at the withers	22–22.5 in. (56–57 cm)	21.5–22 in. (55–56 cm)

The height at the withers in the breed standard should ensure that the Labrador Retriever remains a medium-sized dog. In its proportions, the dog is harmonious with a rectangular silhouette. The distance from withers to sternum should be the same as the length of the leg (distance from elbow to the ground), with a ratio of 1 : 1.

Behavior and Temperament

BREED STANDARD

Good-tempered, very agile. Excellent nose, soft mouth; keen lover of water. Adaptable, devoted companion. Intelligent, keen, and biddable, with a strong will to please. Kindly nature, with no trace of aggression or undue shyness.

On this point the AKC standard is more extensive, where we read that the true Labrador Retriever temperament is as much a hallmark of the breed as the otter tail. The ideal disposition is a kindly, outgoing, tractable nature; eager to please and non-aggressive towards human or animal. The Labrador has much that appeals to people; their gentle ways, intelligence, and adaptability make them an ideal dog. Aggressiveness towards humans or other animals, or any evidence of shyness in an adult, should be severely penalized in competitions.

Coat and Color

BREED STANDARD

Coat: The Labrador Retriever has a water-repellent double coat. The outer coat lies close to the body, is short and straight, although a slight wave down the back is also correct; is dense without feathering, giving a fairly hard feel to the touch; and has a soft, dense, weather-resistant undercoat.

The coat of the Labrador Retriever is very characteristic of the breed. It must consist of a thick undercoat and a stiff, hard outer coat; it is not a soft show coat that is not water-repellent. The hair length is also important: the longer the hairs, the more feathering (fringe) and the chance of a wavy coat, which are undesirable characteristics.

BREED STANDARD

Color: Wholly black, yellow, or chocolate. Small white spot on chest permissible. Yellows range from light cream to fox red with variations in the shadings on ears, under parts, hocks, and down the back. Chocolates range from light sedge to dark chocolate.

The Labrador Retriever must be single-colored, although with yellow and brown coats, shades from light to dark are possible. Yellow dogs usually have a light undercoat. The UKC standard adds the following: "A small white spot on the chest is permissible but not preferred. White hairs from aging or scarring should not be penalized."

The Labrador Retriever is under threat by mixed-breed dogs that have unusual coat colors such as silver, charcoal, champagne, lilac, and others. These mixed-breed dogs will also often show incorrect pigmentation on the nose, eyelids, and sometimes soles of the feet (e.g., a lilac with a brown nose). Some lack the breed's characteristic double coat.

Some breeders, especially in the United States, sell light-colored yellow puppies as a "white" Labrador Retriever or chocolates with

THE BREED STANDARD

Figure 3.2 The three officially recognized coat colors of the Labrador Retriever (from front to back): yellow from light cream to fox red, completely black, and chocolate from light sedge to dark chocolate.

the dilution factor as "silver" Labradors, very often in order to charge higher fees. The silver color is non-standard and would disqualify them as show dogs. Some speculate that the silver Labrador is a result of cross-breeding chocolate Labradors with the Weimaraner. To date, silver Labradors have not appeared outside of the United States by the breeding of two chocolate Labs. The US-based kennel where silver Labradors first appeared also breeds with other gun dogs, including Weimaraners, but the origin of silver Labradors is unclear and the focus of much contention.

All the kennel clubs agree that the only acceptable Labrador Retriever coat colors, as recognized in the official breed standard,

Figure 3.3 The Labrador Retriever is under threat by mixed-breed dogs that pass on non-standard coat colors, such as this silver.

"are black, yellow and chocolate. Any other color or a combination of colors is a disqualification."

Head, Skull, and Muzzle

BREED STANDARD

Head: A kindly, gentle expression is characteristic of the breed. The head is proportionate to the size of the dog, clean-cut, and free from fleshy cheeks. When viewed from the side, the skull and muzzle are approximately equal in length, and joined by a moderate stop that is defined, in part, by the moderately well-defined supraorbital arches over the eyes. A wedge-shape head, or a head long and narrow in muzzle and back skull is incorrect, as is a massive, cheeky head. The jaws are powerful and free from snipiness.

Skull: The skull should be broad; well developed but without exaggeration. The skull and foreface should be on parallel planes and of approximately equal length. There should be a moderate stop — the brow slightly pronounced so that the skull is not absolutely in a straight line with the nose. The brow ridges aid in defining the stop.

Muzzle: Of medium length, powerful, not snipey. Viewed from the top or the side, the muzzle is slightly deeper and wider at the stop than at the tip. Nose wide; nostrils well developed. The nose should be black on black or yellow dogs, and brown on chocolates. Nose color fading to a lighter shade is not a fault. A thoroughly pink nose or one lacking in any pigment is a disqualification. Lips should not be squared off or pendulous, but fall away in a curve toward the throat.

The head has a wide skull. There is a clear stop (transition between nose and skull). The muzzle must be about the same length as the skull. The forenose is large. The muzzle may be only a fraction less deep at the forenose than at the corners of the lips. The lips are rounded and well fitting: the Labrador Retriever is not a drooler.

If the muzzle is narrow and has a tapered tip, it is described as "snipey." If, on the other hand, the muzzle is very broad and too short, and the skull has highly developed jaw muscles (cheeks), the head is described as "mastiff-like." Both are atypical for Labs. The skull and muzzle must be in balance, and the scalp must be smooth and without wrinkles.

a. Correct head with a clear stop and jaws free from snipiness.

b. Not enough stop.

c. Snipey snout.

Figure 3.4 The head of the Labrador Retriever.

Pigmentation on the nose (also on the eyelids and the soles of feet) has to be black for black and yellow Labs; brown or liver on chocolate Labs. Pigmentation fading to a lighter shade on yellows is not penalized.

Jaws and Teeth

BREED STANDARD

Jaws of medium length; jaws and teeth strong with a perfect, regular and complete scissor bite (i.e., upper teeth closely overlapping lower teeth and set square to the jaws).

The teeth are important tools for the work of a retrieving dog. The permanent teeth of a dog include the following:
- **Upper jaw:** 6 upper incisors, 2 canines, 8 premolars and 4 molars (20 teeth total)
- **Lower jaw:** 6 lower incisors, 2 canines, 8 premolars and 6 molars (22 teeth total)

All teeth should have a good size and be clean.

Upper jaw (total)
6 incisors (I_1, I_2, and I_3)
2 canines (C)
8 premolars (P_1, P_2, P_3, and P_4)
4 molars (M_1 and M_2)
= 20 teeth total

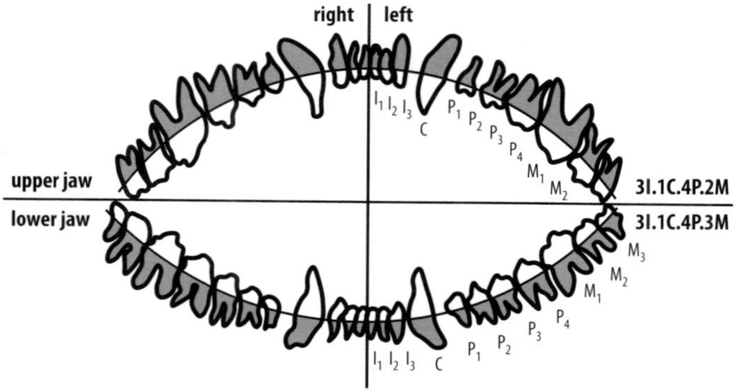

3I.1C.4P.2M
3I.1C.4P.3M

Lower jaw (total)
6 incisors (I_1, I_2, and I_3)
2 canines (C)
8 premolars (P_1, P_2, P_3, and P_4)
6 molars (M_1, M_2, and M_3)
= 22 teeth total

Figure 3.5 Permanent teeth of an adult dog. For simplicity, only one half of the upper and lower jaw are labeled; the left side is a mirror of the right.

The Labrador Retriever must have a *scissor bite* (i.e., with a closed mouth, the incisors of the upper jaw just overlap the incisors of the lower jaw, as with humans). Deviant dentures include the following:
- **Level bite:** the incisor teeth fit together like pincers, so the upper and lower incisors meet exactly, surface to surface
- **Overshot bite:** there is too much space between the incisors of the upper jaw and the incisors of the lower jaw
- **Undershot bite:** the incisors of the lower jaw are in front of the incisors of the upper jaw
- **Crossbite:** the rows of cutting teeth are not parallel, but cross each other. One half therefore closes correctly, but the other half does not.

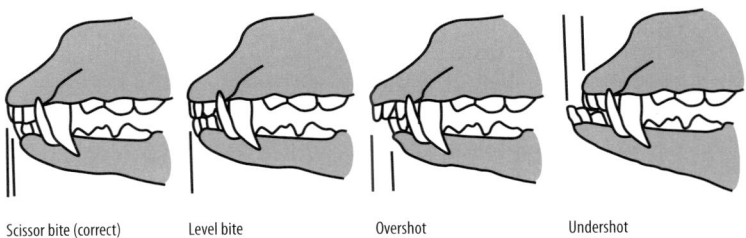

Scissor bite (correct)　　Level bite　　Overshot　　Undershot

Figure 3.6 The different positions of the teeth.

The Labrador Retriever should have a complete set of teeth, which is important for the following reasons:
- Dogs with a complete set of teeth, in which all premolars are present, have to hold their prey less firmly when fetching than with a set of teeth in which premolars are missing. Imagine the row of teeth on a hair comb with some teeth missing. This comb gives you much less grip on your hair than with a complete comb.
- The roots of the molars help strengthen the jaw. Without this strength, both jawbone and gums weaken.

Eyes

BREED STANDARD

Medium size, expressing intelligence and good temper; almond or diamond shape, not round; color dark brown or hazel.

The eyes of the Labrador Retriever give the dog a soft, intelligent, good tempered expression. If the dog's eyes are too light, its expression becomes hard, especially with a black dog. At the same time, dark, almost black eyes give too little expression. Although the eyes of a chocolate Labrador Retriever will never be as dark as those of a yellow or black Lab, the eyes on a chocolate must also be as dark as possible.

The eyeball must not be too deep in the eye sockets and cannot protrude. An eye that is too deep in the eye socket shows smaller than medium size. A bulging (larger) eye is more vulnerable because the eyelids and socket fit less well around the eyeball. A dog with a deep-set eye, on the other hand, has overly large eyelids. These can predispose the dog for entropion and/or ectropion, especially if the dog is generally too loose in the skin. With entropion, the eyelid, above or below, turns inward and the hairs normally found on the upper eyelid touch the eye. The hairs that touch the eyeball cause irritation, inflammation, and damage. With ectropion, the lower eyelid is open, and we see the pink mucosa. This exposure allows dust and sand into the eye, causing inflammation of the eye mucosa.

Ears

BREED STANDARD

The ears of the Labrador Retriever should hang moderately close to the head, set rather far back, and somewhat low on the skull; slightly above eye level. Ears should not be large and heavy, but in proportion with the skull; ears should reach to the inside of the eye when pulled forward.

The ears should reach approximately to the inside corner of the eye when pulled forward. They must be supple and placed far back on the head. Such ears are not as easily damaged in tight undergrowth as large, heavy ears may be. With an attentive-looking dog, well-placed ears do not rise above the skull. Ears placed too low may make the skull appear somewhat convex.

Neck

BREED STANDARD

Clean, strong, medium length, good reach; set into well-placed shoulders.

The neck should be muscular and free from throatiness. It should rise strongly from the shoulders with a moderate arch. The neck must be an effective length to be able to carry heavy prey. A long, elegant neck is therefore unsuitable. An overly short neck or a "ewe" neck (a condition in which the neck is straight and sagging rather than arched), is also incorrect, because the dog in gallop or trot must be able to easily bring their nose to the ground to follow a trail. This is not possible if the neck is too short.

a. Correct shoulder, longer neck

b. Steep shoulder, shorter neck

Figure 3.7 A correct neck length gives the Labrador the optimal strength to carry prey and do nose work.

Forequarters

BREED STANDARD

General appearance: Forelegs straight from elbow to ground when viewed from either front or side.

Shoulder: Long and sloping.
Forearm: Forelegs well boned and straight.

The forequarters consists of the front legs and shoulders. A long, oblique shoulder blade has contact with the rib wall underneath and therefore has a better connection to the muscles that hold it in place (a dog has no clavicle). In addition, this creates a beautiful, smooth neckline. Optimal angulation of the forequarters is essential for good movement. In a normally built dog, which can trot well, the angle that the shoulder blade makes with the vertical line is about 30 degrees, and the angle of the shoulder blade and the upper arm (scapula and humerus) is about 90 degrees.

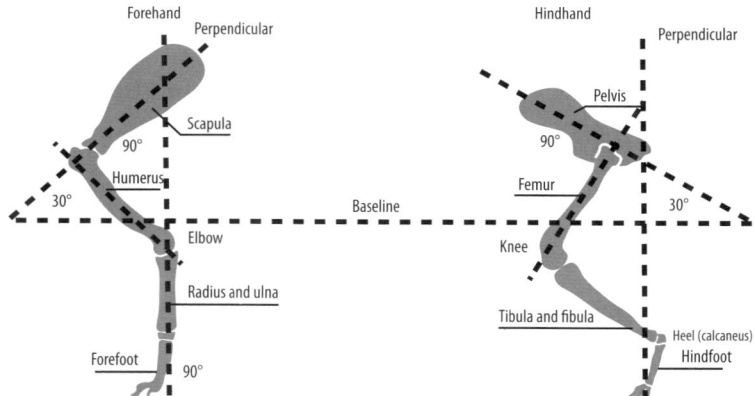

Figure 3.8 The ideal scapula should be long and sloping and should form an angle of approximately 30° angle with the baseline, giving a slightly more than right angle between the scapula and humerus; the dog is then optimally angulated. A similar balance occurs in the hindquarters.

The front legs must be below the deepest point of the sternum in order to support the dog's center of gravity. If you draw an imaginary perpendicular line through the scapula, it should end up in the metacarpal, the large cushion on the sole of the foot. The center of gravity lies somewhere on this vertical line. Where that is exactly depends on the mass of the dog. When the

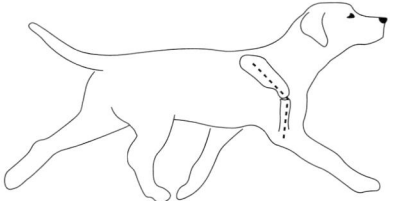 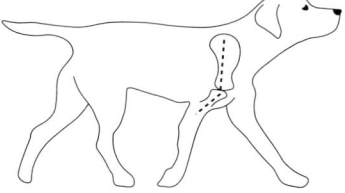

a. Good angulation of the scapula facilitates a long stride and resilience.

b. Poor angulation of the scapula shortens the stride. The dog walks stiffly because it can't extend its front legs properly.

Figure 3.9 Angulation of the scapula impacts how well the dog moves.

center of gravity is supported, the body is in balance and does not require extra energy. If, however, this imaginary line is farther backwards, then extra muscle tension and leverage must be used to bear the dog's weight.

Although the forechest (the anterior part of the chest) is not mentioned in the breed standard, a Labrador should have a well-placed forehand and a deep chest, a sternum that protrudes clearly in front of both shoulder joints.

A Labrador must have good bones. That does not mean, however, that they must have very heavy bones, which would make them clumsy. A dog with legs that are too fine, on the other hand, often has too little mass, which is a handicap when working in dense vegetation. A Labrador Retriever should have straight legs. The front pastern (the part between the wrists and forefoot) is slightly curved and serves as a shock absorber, along with the toes and sole of the foot.

The shoulder position is of great importance for good movement. However, it is difficult to clearly see the position of the shoulder blade during walking. The angulation can vary under different circumstances, not only during prolonged exertion, but also by the way in which the neck is held up and the manner in which the spine is curved. In practice and when hunting, the placement of the shoulder is extremely important for retrieving work (i.e., for picking up and carrying the game). In dogs that are used for hunting, we rarely see bad shoulders. Automatic selection takes place here; after all, dogs with good shoulders can fetch better and quicker. With a steep shoulder position, picking up the game will require a much greater effort by the neck muscles (see Figure 3.10). This is often accompanied by a hard mouth, which can cause the dog to damage the game.

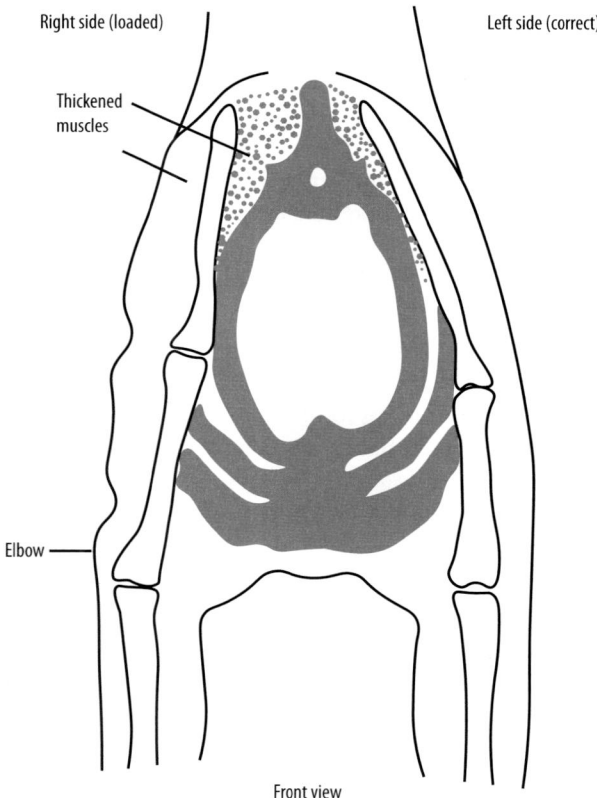

Figure 3.10 Loaded shoulders, often accompanied by a steep scapula position. The scapula position requires the shoulder muscles to over-develop, which in turn causes muscles inside of the shoulder blade to thicken, pushing the tips of the scapula out. The dog will stand wide in front with elbows turned outward.

Body

BREED STANDARD

Topline: Level.

Loin: Wide, short-coupled and strong.

Chest: Of good width and depth, with well-sprung barrel ribs. The FCI standard adds to the last point: "This effect not to be produced by carrying excessive weight."

The body of the Labrador Retriever is broad and deep (the chest reaches to the elbows) with barrel-shaped ribs. However, broad does not mean the wider the better. If a big hand fits between the two front legs, the dog is wide enough. The front ribs are slightly flatter to allow a good connection between the shoulder blades and the elbows. The largest curvature of the ribs is behind the forequarters. The ribs reach far backwards and downwards, so that the line of the belly is only slightly upwards.

The standard prescribes short loins, but these should not be too short, because that makes the dog less agile. A female may be

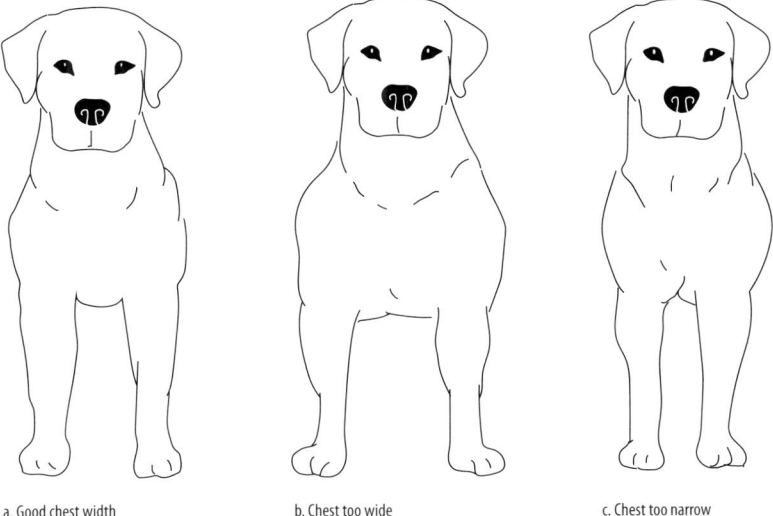

a. Good chest width   b. Chest too wide   c. Chest too narrow

Figure 3.11 Viewed from the front, the Labrador Retriever's chest should be quite wide, but not too wide.

slightly longer in the loins so that there is enough space for the pups during pregnancy.

A horizontal topline does not mean that the back has to be as flat as a plank. After all, the spinal column is a slightly arched, flexible connection between the forequarters and hindquarters.

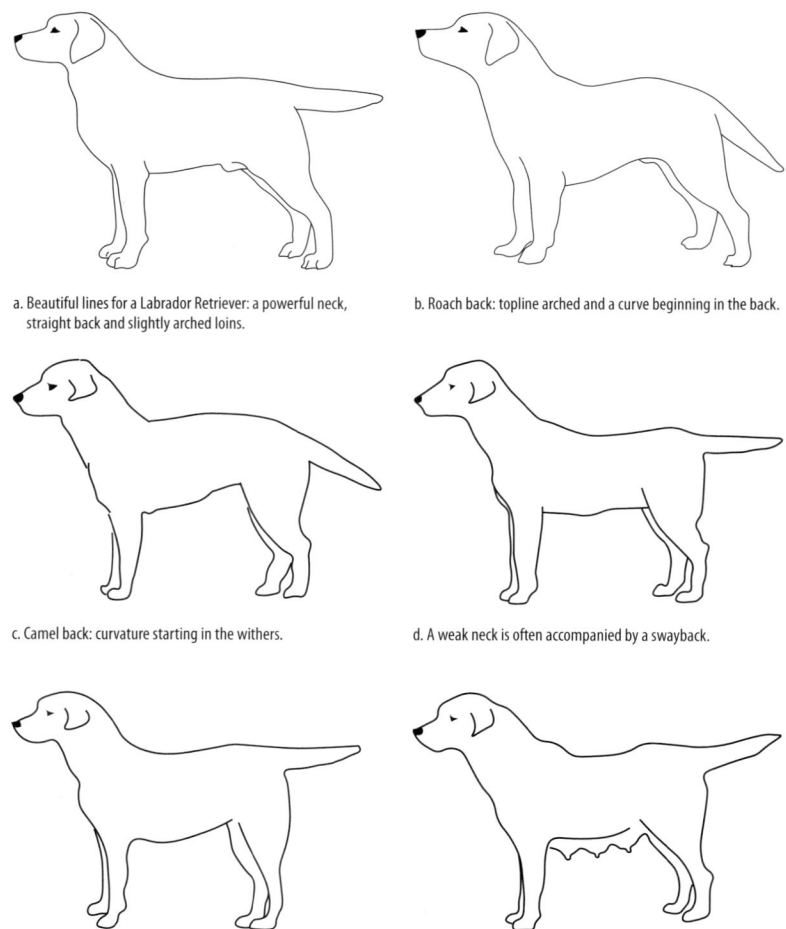

a. Beautiful lines for a Labrador Retriever: a powerful neck, straight back and slightly arched loins.

b. Roach back: topline arched and a curve beginning in the back.

c. Camel back: curvature starting in the withers.

d. A weak neck is often accompanied by a swayback.

e. The croup is higher than the withers; this dog is overbuilt.

f. A dip in the back of an over-used breeding bitch.

Figure 3.12 The lines of the Labrador Retriever.

The impression of a flat back is created by the muscles and coat. The back must be powerful, so not sagged in the middle (swayback or dipped back) or pulled up in the loins (roach back). These abnormalities can be caused by overweight at a young age.

The characteristic construction of barrel-shaped ribs, good musculature, thick coat, and rounded (otter) tail gives the Labrador its typical strong appearance. This cannot be simulated by letting the dog accumulate a thick layer of fat. The only thing you achieve by that is that the dog spoils its back, wrists, and feet, not to mention its movement.

Hindquarters

BREED STANDARD
General appearance: Well-developed hindquarters, not sloping to tail.
Stifle (knee): Well turned.
Metatarsus (back pastern): Hocks well let down. Cowhocks highly undesirable.

There is a big difference in function between the forehand and the hindhand. While the forehand tries to maintain the normal center of gravity, the hindhand propels the dog forward, a motion that is transferred to the forehand via the back, creating the locomotion.

The hindquarters consist of the hind legs and pelvis. The hindquarters must have good musculature and be well angled. In a dog that is correctly positioned with a well-angled hindquarters, if you drew an imaginary perpendicular line from the point of the buttock (point of the ischium) to the ground (Figure 3.8), this line would coincide with the front of the back pastern. A deviating position in the hindquarters, such as cowhocks (back legs showing an X shape), has an adverse effect on the movement. If the pelvis angle to the baseline is too steep or too flat, the dog's hindleg won't have optimal mobility and the dog won't have optimal movement.

Feet

BREED STANDARD
Round, compact; well-arched toes and well-developed pads.

For a hunting dog, well-shaped feet are very important. These should be round like those of a cat, and not too small, but compact, with strongly curved toes, thick pads, and short nails.

Deviant shapes are splay feet, caused by sagging toes, as well as hare feet with an elongated shape because of long middle toes. A paw print in the wet sand will clearly show the model of your dog's foot.

Tail

BREED STANDARD
Distinctive feature, very thick towards base, gradually tapering towards tip, medium length, free from feathering, but clothed thickly all round with a short, thick, dense coat, thus giving the "rounded" appearance described as "otter" tail. May be carried gaily but should not curl over back.

The tail is described quite extensively in the standard because this is such an important characteristic of the Labrador. A good otter tail is rolled, densely hairy, has no flag (feathering) at the bottom like the Golden Retriever, and reaches roughly to the heels. The tail tip is also round and covered with dense hair.

According to the standard, the tail may be worn cheerfully, but it may not curl over the back. A happy tail is thus inclined upwards or is bent slightly upwards, in an extension of the back. The CKC standard adds the following: "Tail may be carried 'happily' but not at more than a 35-degree angle with the back. Tail an extension of the topline and balances the dog." The UKC standard adds this point: "When the dog is relaxed, the tail hangs down naturally. When the dog is moving or alert, the tail may be carried level with the back or only slightly above level. The tail should never curl over the back or be carried between the legs."

Gait/Movement

BREED STANDARD
Free, covering adequate ground; straight and true in front and rear.

Figure 3.13 The otter tail is a distinguishing feature of the Labrador Retriever.

The standards of the KC and the FCI give only this short information, whereas the UKC standard continues with the following:

> When trotting, the gait is effortless, smooth, powerful and well coordinated, showing good but not exaggerated reach in front and drive behind. When moving, the dog's head moves

forward so that the head, backline, and tail are nearly even. The topline remains level with only a slight flexing to indicate suppleness. Viewed from any position, legs turn neither in nor out, nor do feet cross or interfere with each other. As speed increases, feet tend to converge toward the center line of balance. It is recommended that dogs be shown on a loose lead and moved at a moderate speed to reflect true gait. Poor movement should be penalized to the degree to which it reduces the Labrador Retriever's ability to perform the tasks it was bred to do.

The AKC standard gives the most information about gait and movement:

Movement of the Labrador Retriever should be free and effortless. When watching a dog move toward oneself, there should be no sign of elbows out. Rather, the elbows should be held neatly to the body with the legs not too close together. Moving straight forward without pacing or weaving, the legs should form straight lines, with all parts moving in the same plane. Upon viewing the dog from the rear, one should have the impression that the hind legs move as nearly as possible in a parallel line with the front legs. The hocks should do their full share of the work, flexing well, giving the appearance of power and strength. When viewed from the side, the shoulders should move freely and effortlessly, and the foreleg should reach forward close to the ground with extension. A short, choppy movement or high knee action indicates a straight shoulder; paddling indicates long, weak pasterns; and a short, stilted rear gait indicates a straight rear assembly; all are serious faults. Movement faults interfering with performance, including weaving; side-winding; crossing over; high knee action; paddling; and short, choppy movement, should be severely penalized.

A hunting dog must be able to move smoothly. In principle, a correctly built dog should be able to walk well, but due to, among other things, incorrect training, excess weight, or weak muscles, various deviations can occur. An improperly built dog has predictable deviations in its movement. The body always tries to compensate for the shortcomings.

The most serious obstacles to the gait are pinched elbows and cowhocks. *Pinched elbows* means the elbows bend towards each other and the feet angle out; this condition is clearly visible when looking at the dog from the front. *Cowhocks* is a similar condition

Figure 3.14 If the forequarters and hindquarters are both correctly constructed, we see a nice balance in the body, known as "static balance." We also see balance in the gait and the stride lengths, in which the feet of the hindquarters are placed where the feet of the forequarters left the ground. The dog will have a nice, flat topline without up and down fluctuations.

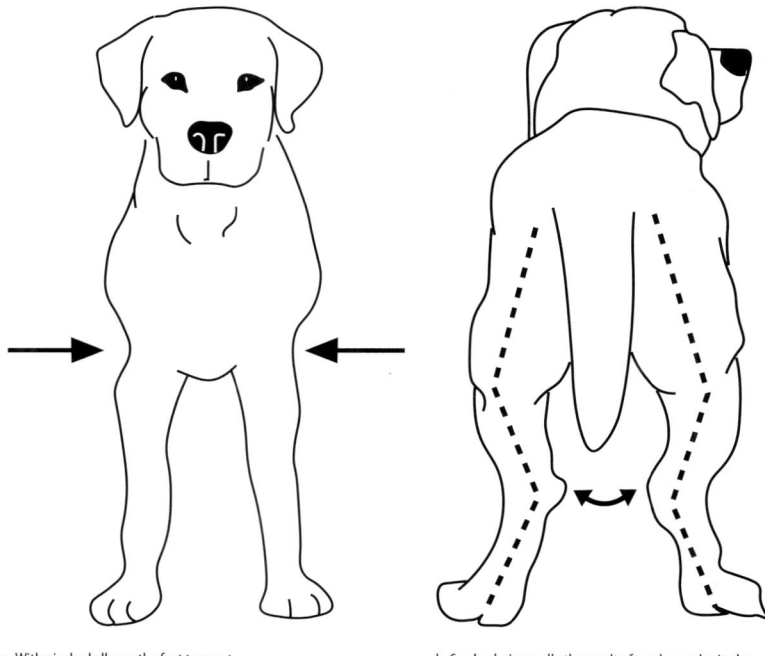

a. With pinched elbows the feet turn out.

b. Cowhocks is usually the result of weak muscles in the hindquarters.

Figure 3.15 Pinched elbows and cowhocks are both serious faults that hinder the dog's movement.

for the back legs, in which the hocks turn in and the hind feed point out. Both are serious mistakes causing the dog to move more slowly than optimal, and requiring more effort and propulsion to move. It makes little difference if the dog has well-muscled hindquarters if it is cowhocked. The condition means the dog's momentum will not be optimally converted into a forward movement, but will largely be lost laterally.

Conclusion

Labrador Retrievers that meet the breed standard in construction and character are ideal working dogs, always enthusiastic to carry out their tasks. With their good nose and soft mouth, they are excellent retrieving gun dogs to hunt waterfowl or upland game for long hours under difficult conditions. They also excel in all performance activities as a service dog, are extremely intelligent, and are easily trained to perform a variety of complex tasks.

4

Training the Labrador Retriever

The Labrador Retriever temperament is as much a hallmark of the breed as the otter tail. The ideal disposition is kindly, outgoing, and tractable, eager to please and not aggressive towards human or animal. The Labrador has much that appeals to people; their gentle ways, intelligence, and adaptability make them an ideal dog.

Many of the Labrador Retriever's features stem from its role as a hunting dog. Labs are friendly to other dogs; after all, they had to cooperate with many other dogs on the hunting fields. And as a gun dog they had to be pleasing and adaptable because they had to be able to work with many different hunters. It was and still is common for a retriever to be loaned to fellow hunters.

Because also in the past people did not want to spend too much time training dogs, it was a plus if the dog wanted to please the hunter. This "will to please" is now one of the nicest qualities when training and working with a Labrador.

The steadiness needed in a hunting dog has ensured that the Labrador Retriever is stable. Steadiness means the dog will sit quietly next to someone, even if people start shooting nearby, and hares jump up and run away right in front of it.

The Labrador Retriever has been said to be "an Englishman in heart and soul." Labs are dignified and rarely rude or noisy as adults. In their upbringing they do not need a hard hand, but

Figure 4.1 It is common for a retriever to be loaned out for a hunting party. The breed is adaptable and willing to work with multiple handlers.

Figure 4.2 Humans sometimes marvel at how much the Labrador loves to retrieve a ball, but perhaps he retrieves it because he thinks we like to throw it!

they do, of course, need clear guidelines. They are very friendly to children.

Labrador Retriever breeders have developed separate field and show lines. Field line Labrador Retrievers have been bred with an emphasis on hunting abilities, and show line Labradors have been bred with an emphasis on conformation and temperament. Dogs from field lines will generally have a lot of drive and will often exhibit more energy, although show people sometimes claim that field lines do not much look like Labradors anymore and lack the correct temperament.

Training Basics

Labrador Retrievers are outstanding working dogs for nose work. Scent detection is their job, and it is easy to train them into excellent search dogs because they have a good ball drive and are very interested in food as a reward. Their nose, disposition, and trainability make them particularly suitable for these types of activities, and the breed has a distinguished history in these endeavors.

Figure 4.3 The Labrador Retriever is an outstanding working dog, especially for nose work, as this 11-week old puppy demonstrates, indicating his toy between the flowers.

Labradors are not reliable guards, although some can be protective, and most will bark if they hear or see something they don't like, especially if it is near their yard.

Labrador Retrievers develop late and often do not reach full maturity until they turn at least two years of age. On the other hand, they retain their abilities to old age and have been known to work well even at 10 years of age.

Figure 4.4 Labrador Retrievers as a breed develop late and often do not reach full maturity until they are two years old.

Labradors are active dogs, especially in puppyhood, and due to their rather late maturity, you will have a dog that is mentally a puppy, with a puppy's energy, up to around the age of three. Labrador puppies are sometimes labeled hyperactive when they are simply normal, exuberant, bouncy young dogs. If you are prepared to deal with this period of time in their life, you will not have problems.

Labrador Retrievers have a reputation for enthusiastic eating, and individuals have been described as willing to eat "anything that isn't nailed down." They are also persuasive and persistent in requesting food. For this reason, the Labrador owner must carefully control the dog's food intake to avoid obesity and its associated health problems. A healthy Labrador Retriever should keep a very slight hourglass waist and be fit and lithe, rather than fat or heavy-set. Excessive weight is a risk factor in the later development of hip dysplasia and diabetes and also can contribute to general reduced health when older. Arthritis is commonplace in older, overweight Labs.

Training Labrador Retrievers with food is easy, but it can also be dangerous if it leads to excess weight. Only use food as a reward if you deduct it from the dog's normal daily portion of food. Training with a ball as a reward is a good alternative. Most Labrador Retrievers enjoy retrieving a ball endlessly.

Labs are considerably fun-oriented and open-minded to new things. They thrive on human attention and interaction and rarely get enough. Reflecting their retrieving bloodline, almost every Lab loves going into water and swimming.

How Dogs Learn

Labs are easy to train and normally very obedient. As a rule they are not excessively prone to territorialism, pining, insecurity, aggression, destructiveness, hypersensitivity, or other difficult traits. But some lines, particularly those bred specifically for their working ability rather than for show, are particularly fast and athletic. Their fun-loving boisterousness and lack of fear can sometimes result in mischief. These active dogs, in particular, require training and firm handling at times to ensure the mischief-making does not get out of hand. Here we have to speak with an iron fist in a velvet glove: in a gentle, careful, but determined fashion. Establish clear rules and consistent handling without physical harshness.

Compulsion training is absolutely not necessary for dogs nowadays. Modern training techniques help us teach dogs exercises and allow them to learn easily. In the case of dog training, there are three important types of learning we will discuss here: classical (Pavlovian) conditioning, operant conditioning, and habituation.

Figure 4.5 Modern training techniques help us teach dogs what we want and allow them to learn easily.

Today, most dog trainers employ classical (Pavlovian) conditioning and operant conditioning. Dogs perform well when they are trained using these methods, and they learn very quickly which behaviors bring them rewards and pleasure. The third type of learning — habituation — begins from the moment a dog is born. Through habituation, dogs learn what parts of their environment to pay attention to and what to ignore. (You can read more about modern methods of dog training in Resi Gerritsen, Ruud Haak, and Simon Prins's *K9 Behavior Basics: A Manual for Proven Success in Operational Service Dog Training*.)

To be a successful dog handler, you not only have to develop a good relationship with your Labrador Retriever, but you must also understand how dogs learn. For example, your dog needs *immediate* feedback about his actions in order for him to understand what he has done well (or not well). A dog that has demolished the seats of the car and then fallen asleep will not understand what the owner is shouting about when the owner returns to the car. Immediate feedback is crucial to a dog's understanding of his actions, and it is at the base of the following types of conditioning.

Figure 4.6 To be a successful dog handler, you not only have to develop a good relationship with your Labrador Retriever, but you also must understand how dogs learn.

CLASSICAL CONDITIONING

When you employ classical conditioning, your dog learns that there is a relationship between two stimuli. One stimulus is called "neutral" or "conditioned" and is usually represented by the sound of a clicker or bell. Normally a dog does not pay attention to the noise emitted by the conditioned stimulus, so called because only as a result of conditioning will this stimulus generate a behavior. The other stimulus, "unconditioned," is biologically important to a dog and is usually represented by food. For example, dogs will pay attention to food without being taught to do so.

Russian physiologist Ivan Pavlov discovered the power of conditioned and unconditioned stimuli accidentally during a study with a dog. He placed a dog on a table, and then he rang a bell, after which he immediately gave the dog food. After repeating this exercise a few times, Pavlov discovered that ringing the bell made the dog salivate: in the dog's mind, the ringing bell predicted food. Today, trainers often use a clicker (rather than Pavlov's bell) and food or another reward, such as a ball, when they wish to employ classical conditioning to train a dog. Labrador Retrievers trained in this method quickly learn that a click sound ushers in a reward of some kind.

OPERANT CONDITIONING

When using operant conditioning, you use four methods to influence your dog's behavior:

1. Positive reinforcement
2. Negative reinforcement
3. Positive punishment
4. Negative punishment

POSITIVE REINFORCEMENT

If we want a dog to behave a certain way more often, we use positive reinforcement by giving the dog something it likes when it behaves that way, thereby increasing the likelihood that the dog will behave that way again. For instance, if you want your Labrador Retriever to sit, you give him a treat as soon as he sits. He will sit more often because he likes receiving a treat.

NEGATIVE REINFORCEMENT

Negative reinforcement can also be used to increase the likelihood that a behavior will occur again. Instead of adding something positive to the dog's environment (the treat, in the example above), you introduce something the dog perceives as negative. For example, if you want to stop your dog's barking, you could make a terrible noise as soon as barking commences and only stop when the barking stops. Negative reinforcement is the principle behind stop-barking e-collars: when a dog wearing such a collar barks, it is either subjected to an unpleasant smell or is shocked by an electrical impulse. The moment the dog stops barking, the unpleasant smell or shock stops. Sometimes, however, the deployment of negative reinforcement is not always clear enough for the dog to learn what the desired behavior is, and it doesn't always result in the change of behavior that we want.

POSITIVE PUNISHMENT

With positive punishment, you add something aversive to your dog's environment to discourage a behavior: an unexpected, unpleasant noise when the dog barks, for example. Because it surprises and annoys the dog, the noise will cause the dog to stop barking. As he learns that the noise starts up every time he barks, the dog will bark less to avoid hearing the noise. As well, a handler might discourage a dog from chasing other dogs (or rabbits or other animals) by throwing a rattling chain on the dog's back as soon as he starts to chase. In similar circumstances, some handlers put an e-collar around the dog's neck and shock the dog as soon as he starts a chase, or they put the dog in a prong or pinch collar with a long leash attached to a pole, so the collar closes automatically as soon as he runs away. This type of punishment was often used in early days of dog training, and some trainers and handlers continue to employ such methods even though they are quite unnecessary. Happily, some countries now forbid the use of prong or pinch collars and e-collars.

NEGATIVE PUNISHMENT

The last method used in operant conditioning to decrease the frequency of certain behaviors is negative punishment: removing something your Labrador Retriever experiences as pleasurable. For example, if you do not want your dog to jump up on you, do not pay attention to him when he jumps. If he tries to get your attention in a way you do not like, ignore him until he behaves in a way you do like. Once he does, then give your dog lots of attention to reinforce the good behavior.

HABITUATION

From the moment your Labrador Retriever was born, he has been surrounded by stimuli that he must get used to and learn from. He soon learns to distinguish between the sounds, smells, sights, and tactile stimuli that he should attend to and those that are not important. After all, any organism's nervous system would be overloaded if it reacted to all environmental stimuli. For example, imagine that every day at 10:00 a.m., a courier drops a package on a porch and honks his horn to alert the homeowner. A dog living in that neighborhood hears the honk every day, but no one in his house ever gets a delivery. When the dog first heard the honk, he barked, but after a while, he noticed that nobody in the house reacted to the sound, so he dismissed the honk as unimportant. For that dog, the courier's honk caused neither an aversive nor a pleasurable response; he just became used to it. You can make use of habituation in two ways when you are teaching your Labrador Retriever: by either flooding or desensitizing your dog.

When flooding, you present a stimulus with no corresponding response from you until your dog stops reacting to it. In this way, he learns to ignore the stimulus because the stimulus has no consequences.

When desensitizing, you first present the stimulus at a low level and then gradually raise the level of the stimulus. When your Labrador Retriever is habituated to the stimulus, he will be desensitized: all experiences of the stimulus (from low to high) will not provoke a response. For example, some Labrador Retrievers are trained using desensitization to ignore the sound of a shotgun. You begin by exposing your dog to the sound of a shot fired far away, perhaps when you are playing with your dog. Then you gradually decrease the distance from which the shot is fired until your helper can shoot close to your dog and not provoke a response.

We also use habituation when training dogs for obedience. For example, when teaching your Labrador Retriever to sit, you begin by choosing a training space that lacks distractions: a room in your house or in your garden. When your dog has practiced the exercise a few times, you can move the "classroom" to a place where there are more distractions, such as a dog-training center at a time when dogs are absent. (The smell of other dogs is a distraction, even if they are not present.) If your dog is able to perform the exercise correctly every time when the training center is quiet, then try taking him there to train when other dogs are present. Gradually increase distractions until your dog ignores them.

The Importance of Clear Signals

Dogs learn skills best when they are offered rewards such as treats, a game of ball or tug, or even permission to repeat a behavior or trick that the dog likes to perform. In addition to giving rewards, you should use cue words. The cue word could be "Yes," "Good," or "Free," or you may instead use a clicker. This tells your Lab that he has done well. In the beginning, rewards should immediately follow appropriate behavior. The combination of

Figure 4.7 The combination of clear and consistent cue words and rewards helps dogs learn when they are doing the right things.

clear and consistent cue words and rewards help dogs learn when they are doing the right things. The need to communicate clear signals during training is incredibly important and cannot be stressed enough.

When teaching any exercise, it is important that you give a command only once; if the dog does not follow, then the handler must help with the execution at the second command. If the dog were to be given a second, third, or fourth whistle or command with the handler waiting each time for the dog to respond, the dog learns that he can decide for himself when he will respond.

By calling the dog's name before giving a command, the dog learns that the command given after his name is meant for him. If training with several dogs, a thrown dummy and the command "Fetch" can be sufficient to break all the dogs. But the dog who has learned to obey only after first hearing his name will stay tidy.

CLEVER HANS CUES

Everyone who has ever tried to teach a dog something knows that dogs respond very well to handler cues. Dogs also pick up cues that they were not specifically trained in. For example, if you put on your walking shoes, your dog will stick to you like glue because he hopes to go for a walk. This is an obvious cue, but your dog will also learn from much subtler cues, even ones that you yourself are completely unconscious of.

These kinds of unconscious cues are called "Clever Hans" cues, based on the apparent mathematic abilities of a horse called Hans, who lived in Germany at the turn of the 20th century. His owner, Wilhelm von Osten, discovered that Hans could count and do sums. Von Osten would ask Hans, "How much is five and two?" and Hans would start tapping his hoof, stopping after seven. This ability led to widespread discussion about the mental abilities of animals in general, until scientists carefully observed von Osten giving Hans sums to do. By watching both von Osten and Hans, and other people giving sums to Hans, Oskar Pfungst deduced that Hans responded to van Osten's slight leaning forward as a cue to stop tapping his hoof when he reached the correct answer.[1]

Figure 4.8 Clever Hans cues are named for a horse with apparent mathematic abilities. He is shown here with his owner and trainer, Wilhelm von Osten.

Another doubter of Hans' abilities was Emilio Rendich, a painter. He had also observed that Hans responded to von Osten's leaning forward and backward and trained his dog Nora to respond in much the same way. The dog would start responding, and when the correct figure was reached, Rendich would lean forward and Nora would stop.[2] Since this time, scientists have studied how dogs quickly pick up cues such as pointing, nodding, glancing, and head bows, even without receiving explicit training to do so.[3]

The significance of these experiments is that they illustrate how well dogs can learn to "read" us. During training, we want dogs to respond only to the relevant cue. So when training a dog to search for an odor, the only cue must be odor. Sometimes handler cues are obvious, even if unintended. We have often seen dogs in scent identification line-up training hovering over each tube, carefully watching their handlers. A minimal movement from a handler is enough for a dog to respond to a tube. The question becomes, how can trainers prevent themselves from cueing the dog in some way, if dogs can pick up and use such minimal signals as just glancing at the matching odor?

The answer is obvious: work "blind." Do not know the position of the matching odor, and preferably have no one close by who knows it, (meaning work so-called "double blind") since even a bystander or helper may unconsciously cue the dog.

TEACHING THE CUE WORD

Before your dog understands the cue word, you must teach it to him by uttering the word in combination with a reward, much like Pavlov's bell and food experiment. Your dog thus learns that the cue word means "Okay, stop, and food." The moment he hears the cue word, he knows he will get a reward. In the beginning, the reward should be food; later, you can reward your dog with a game of ball or tug.

The combination of cue word and reward is a positive one for dogs and worth employing as you take your dog through the obedience exercises. Your dog will want to practice the exercises again and again because of the rewards. For you, the handler, this method is also satisfying because you know you have established a clear channel of communication.

VARIETY IS KEY

It is also important that you do not follow a set pattern in training, day in and day out. Change up the timing of rewards — for example, if you have been working on the Down exercise, change the amount of lying-down time, first 10 minutes, then 3, then 15. Variety is your dog's friend in all training exercises.

Punishment

Sometimes your Labrador Retriever will not do what you want, and so you must correct him. First, ask yourself, "Did I teach my dog this behavior? Is this a behavior that needs to be corrected?" If the answer is yes, you can choose between three methods of punishment: positive punishment, negative punishment, or time out. Correcting dogs by using pinch collars and electronic collars is old fashioned, potentially damaging, and absolutely not recommended in training Labrador Retrievers.

POSITIVE PUNISHMENT

To be effective, positive punishment must be immediate and strong enough to suppress the unwanted behavior. Also, the punishment must be deployed in a way that ensures your dog associates it only with the unwanted behavior. The punishment must elicit a response every time for it to work; that is, your dog must respond to the punishment by stopping the inappropriate behavior. For instance, perhaps your young dog likes playing with other dogs, and while training him the Heeling exercise, he runs to another dog to play. You could at this point grab him by the neck and shake him a bit, and say a very powerful "No."

NEGATIVE PUNISHMENT

Negative punishment gives your dog the opportunity to self-correct. Remember that dogs will do whatever they can to be rewarded. If you notice your Labrador Retriever is not performing an exercise correctly, such as sitting, you can apply negative punishment by withholding a reward and saying "No." After saying "No," say "Sit" again, and if your dog responds correctly, give him the cue word and reward. Your Lab has already learned that the cue word means a reward. If one of his actions does not lead to the cue word and reward, he will try to figure out what he has to do to get the reward again.

TIME OUT

Finally, you can also use a time out to correct your dog's unwanted behavior. This is a good option if your dog is over-stimulated or distracted and is not able to concentrate on the work. However, bear in mind that time outs only work when your dog wants to train. If your dog is already tired and wanting a rest, then the time out will seem like a reward.

Basic Position

In the basic position, the dog sits at the handler's side in a close, straight, calm, and attentive manner, so that his shoulder is at the handler's knee. If you are right-handed, you traditionally train your Labrador Retriever to take the basic position on your left side and also heel at your left side. This is because you would carry a hunting rifle in your right hand, so in order not to bother you, the dog must be on your left side. If you are left-handed, let your Labrador Retriever take the basic position on your right side and also heel at your right side.

There are several methods to teach a dog the correct basic position. Some dog handlers pull the dog's head up with the leash in front and push down with a hand on the dog's back. This forces the dog into the position, but it results in many dogs trying to avoid basic position because they do not like the pulling and pushing. A better method of teaching the position follows.

TRAINING THE BASIC POSITION
1. Start with a piece of food in your left hand and your Labrador Retriever on leash.
2. Take a few steps forward, ensuring your dog sees the food.
3. The dog will move to your left side. Take care that the dog is close to your left leg.
4. Stop walking, keeping your left hand over the head of the dog.
5. He will sit down as he tries to look up and back at your hand.
6. As soon as he sits, give the cue word (e.g., Good, Yes) and the piece of food.
7. Repeat this several times, and then begin saying the command "Heel" or "Sit" the moment your Labrador Retriever sits down. Follow "Heel" or "Sit" immediately with the cue word and then the piece of food. If you only reward the dog when he is in the right position, he always will sit in the right way.

TRAINING HEELING
Once the dog knows the basic position, he is ready to learn heeling.
1. Take some food in your left hand, and walk a half pace forward. Your dog will follow and try to get into the correct basic position in order to have his reward. If he is doing this correctly, give him the cue word and the reward.

Figure 4.9 While walking, hold a piece of food in your left hand to get the dog's attention to follow you. Then stop walking, keeping your left hand over the head of the dog. He will sit down as he tries to look up and back at your hand.

2. Repeat this many times until your dog does it well.
3. For the next stage, take a step to the side and let your dog follow and return to basic position. Give the cue word and reward.
4. Once step 3 is consistent, make a turn of 90 degrees and let your dog follow. Give the cue word and reward.
5. Repeat many times so the dog has a clear understanding about where he has to be. Vary the movements you make.
6. Once your dog consistently follows your single step, start taking two steps. If you've been consistent with your rewards, the dog will stay in the correct position, no matter which way you move.

7. If this goes well, start taking three and four steps. Do not move too quickly, especially at first, to ensure your dog can move alongside you.

In between advances in training difficulty, periodically go back to earlier stages. Take care that you do not advance through the stages too quickly. You want to give the dog a chance to thoroughly learn each step before learning something new.

TIPS FOR SUCCESS
Teach your Labrador Retriever when he is in a low drive. A dog that is too active and energetic is not able to learn well. If you have an active, high-temperament dog, allow him to blow off some steam before training, perhaps by running, playing, or retrieving the ball. Dogs with low or middle temperament can become more focused and more attentive in the heeling once you start using a ball instead of food. High-temperament dogs can become so passionate about retrieving the ball that they can't concentrate on learning new things.

It is very important that the handler never let the training become too routine. The rewards have to be interesting and come at different moments: sometimes during the heeling, sometimes in the basic position. If the reward comes during heeling, then the dog handler has to take care to vary when it is given. Do not always provide the reward after eight steps, for example, or your dog may think he only has to heel until step eight.

Move slowly through training and do not advance to a new lesson until the dog has learned the current lesson. Begin each training session by repeating earlier lessons. If the dog cannot reliably perform earlier lessons in review, do not advance until it can.

Begin training at home, either inside or outside, as long as there are no distractions. As the dog learns each command, you can gradually begin practicing the command in locations with more distractions. For example, you might begin inside, then move to outside, where there are more sights, sounds, and smells that might call for the dog's attention. Eventually, move to the training center when there are no other dogs around. Once the dog has mastered commands in that environment, you can begin training with other dogs and trainers in the area.

PUPPY TRAINING

Puppies and young dogs may need to repeat every training exercise at least 20 times before they are ready for the next step. And those 20 repeats should not be completed in one training session! Each training session should consist of no more than three repeats, and always stop training for the day on a successful note.

Training can start with eight-week-old puppies, but training sessions should be short, only a few minutes, and only three times a week.

Rewards

Use food to teach the start of heeling. In general, food will not make Labs hyperactive, so it is easy to bring the dog into the desired position, and you will likely have his attention.

After your dog shows the correct heeling position consistently, you can begin to reward with a ball or other reward instead of food. You have many rewarding possibilities: balls on rope; magnetic balls, which you can attach to your training vest; soft balls; different types of tugs, and so on. Choose what appeals to your dog since it's his reward. First play with the dog with the ball or tug by moving it very fast and throwing it away and so on. Soon the dog will like the toy very much. Now you can use it in the heeling exercise.

If the dog is able to heel in a straight path for about 10 to 15 steps, you can start training with a different type of reward. Put your Lab in the basic position and very slowly use your right hand to place the ball under your armpit. As soon as your dog looks up and focuses on the ball, give him the cue word and let the ball fall down as a reward for being focused and attentive. If this situation is clear for the dog, take a step and drop the ball, only if, of course, the dog is in the correct heeling position.

With a magnetic ball, the handler places it on their training jacket in several positions, such as behind on the back, high or low. Later in training, the dog can pick the ball from the vest himself after the cue word. The dog handler does not have to make any movement. This method of reward helps guard against the handler giving unconscious clues to the dog in order to give the reward.

Another possibility is to hold a ball in your right hand. After the command "Heel" and the dog has quickly moved into the correct basic position, give the cue word and then throw the ball with your right hand to the left side and behind the dog. This method works well for dogs who are not especially focused in the basic position or who sit too far in front. They will shift their position back because they want to be able to quickly reach the ball.

When you start using a ball reward, always throw it backwards, not forwards in the direction you are moving; otherwise, the dog will heel too far forward. The dog will always try to get the reward as quickly as possible, so he will anticipate your throw and walk ahead of you. If you consistently throw the reward backwards, the dog will not advance ahead.

Shooting Training

All hunting and professional working dogs have to be gun-sure. If you are choosing a puppy out of a litter, it is important to know who the parents are and what they have done in hunting or other working disciplines.

If you are starting with an older Labrador Retriever, test the dog in shooting as soon as possible. For testing, the dog or the puppy can be in a familiar place.

TESTING FOR GUN-SURENESS
1. Have the dog play with the dog handler or somebody else it knows.
2. Have a helper with a gun stand at least 160 feet (50 m) away.
3. At a sign from a person observing the dog, the helper shoots twice, the second shot five seconds after the first.

If the dog does not react at all, everything is good: the dog is gun-sure. If the dog looks up, but immediately continues playing, then you know you have to train for shooting. A dog that stops playing and expresses fear has a problem with the shot. It would be better not to accept this dog for training. Of course, it is sometimes possible to work out shooting shyness, but if the shyness is in the disposition of the dog, training will be difficult. Because you never know exactly where the problem is coming from, it is safer to choose a different dog.

Assuming you have a Labrador Retriever, puppy or older dog, that is rather neutral to the sound of gunshots, start shooting training using the habituation method. This means that during training, you will frequently arrange to have some controlled shooting in the vicinity. In the beginning, the shots are made during play between the handler and dog, until the dog ignores the sound. Later, once the dog knows the heeling exercise, arrange for two shots during heeling. This should be first from a distance of about 130 feet (40 m). Gradually reduce the distance to about 50 feet (15 m) with the dog sitting in the basic position beside the handler.

It is important that the dog associate shooting with the training situation in the field, never during quiet time or at home. Every time the dog is at the field, it knows there are other dogs, other people, and shooting. There is also the ball and the tug. The dog associates shooting with "work time" and no other situation. You don't want the dog thinking shooting could happen at home, or it may be restless, thinking work could begin.

Training on a Table

Several methods can teach dogs to perform the Sit, Down, and Stand exercises. We like to use a table to teach all three of these exercises. The advantage of working on a table is that your Labrador Retriever learns not to move forward when he is assuming a position. The table must be small enough that your Lab will not be able to walk around on it. He should not be able to crawl forward when in the Down position, either. Working on a small tabletop will help your dog learn how to assume the positions without making any unnecessary steps or movements.

Put your puppy or young dog on top of a small table. Make sure he likes the table and feels comfortable there. The table's surface should not be wet or slippery. You may wish to employ a

Figure 4.10 We use a stable table and a clicker to train Labrador Retriever Guus the Sit, Stand, and Down positions.

Figure 4.11 Training has to start young. This 10-week-old chocolate Labrador Retriever demonstrates the Sit exercise.

Figure 4.12 Seamus, the young Labrador Retriever, is trained to Sit and Stay at a distance.

clicker; clicks are faster to execute than cue words, which helps the dog make the correct association of behavior and reward. When you are working with your Labrador Retriever on the tabletop, you will also want to have some food — perhaps a long strip of cheese — in your left hand.

Begin by training Sit, Stand, and Down in one succession. Once the dog knows all three positions, train them separately to avoid routine. Initially, you will use your hand position, a click, and a treat to show the dog what you want. Once the dog knows the positions, you can add in spoken commands.

TRAINING SIT

Once your dog is comfortable on the table, hold your closed left hand with the food above his head. Your thumb and forefinger should be up. Your dog should follow the movement of your hand and sit down. If necessary, move your hand back over your

Figure 4.13 When teaching your Lab to sit on the table, hold a treat above his head as shown. The moment he sits, click and give him the reward. Do not add a command to this training exercise until he understands what is expected of him.

Lab's head a bit until he sits. As soon as he sits down, click the clicker and give your dog some of the food in your hand, but do not yet link a command to the action.

TRAINING STAND
After your dog sits down properly and receives the reward, turn your left hand around in front of his head, and open up your hand a bit. Your dog will stand up, because he wants to eat the rest of the treat out of your hand. As soon as he stands up, click and let your Labrador Retriever eat.

TRAINING DOWN
Do not train your dog to perform the Down position from the Sit position. The dog should learn to lie down in one fluid movement from a standing position. Once he knows the position, you can sometimes have him move from Sit to Down, but do not make this the pattern he learns by.

With your dog in the standing position, palm some food in your left hand, turn your hand so the palm faces down, and open it a bit so your dog could reach the food if he put his nose under your hand. Now, put your hand on the tabletop and move it

Figure 4.14 To encourage your Lab to return to standing, take another treat in hand, hold the hand in front of your dog's head, and open your hand up a bit. Your dog will stand because he wants to eat the treat out of your hand. As soon as he stands up, click, and reward him with the treat.

Figure 4.15 To teach your Lab to lie down from a standing position, palm a treat and then partially close your hand around it. Turn your hand so the back is up (palm down) and open your hand so your dog can reach the treat from underneath. Place your hand down on the table and slide it between your dog's forelegs. He will lie down to get the treat; click and reward him.

between your Lab's forelegs. He will lie down, following the food in your hand, and as soon as he does so, click and give him the reward.

PRACTICE
Repeat these exercises on the table over and over again, but change the sequence of the positions. Avoid training the dog to move from the Sit position into the Down position too often because you do not want your dog to associate Sit with Down and sitting before lying down: Down is its own, distinct movement.

Figure 4.16 To your dog, training becomes an enjoyable game.

COMBINING COMMANDS WITH POSITIONS
1. When you are sure your Labrador Retriever can assume all the positions quickly and with confidence, start speaking the command for the position as soon as he takes the position. The sequence of training events should be as follows: hand movement, command, click, reward. Practice with Sit, Stand, and Down.

2. The next step is to train your dog to maintain each position a bit longer before receiving the food reward.
3. When he can stay in position for a bit before being rewarded, the next step is to take a few steps back from the table while training.
4. Progress by gradually removing your hand signals from the training sequence: from giving the hand signal every time before giving the command, begin giving the command followed by the hand signal. As always, progress slowly, and don't hesitate to backtrack to earlier lessons if your dog starts encountering problems.
5. When your Labrador Retriever only requires your command to take a position, try to change your position relative to him during training. First, work in front of your dog, and then stand at the side of the table with your dog on your left. Then try to give the hand signals from farther and farther away.

When the dog is consistently successful with your tabletop exercises, you may wish to work on only one position at a time so the dog doesn't expect to do all three positions together. Another way to vary the training is to change the reward from food to gently tossing a ball toward him so he can catch it.

Training on the Ground
Although we find table training useful, you may, of course, choose to train your dog on the ground.

TRAINING SIT
Train the Sit position with the dog on your left side with his shoulder blade aligned with your knee (the basic position). Keep the leash short so he cannot move away.
1. Hold a piece of food in your left hand above the dog's head and slowly move your hand backward. The dog will watch your hand and naturally sit in order to follow the hand's progression.
2. Sometimes a dog will need a bit of extra help. With a piece of food in your right hand, move your hand over his head. As you do so, glide your left hand down his back and very gently

encourage his back end down. The movement of your treat-bearing hand in combination with your gliding hand will cause your dog to sit.

3. As soon as he sits, click or say the cue word and then reward your dog with the food. Repeat this several times. He should sit as your right hand moves up and your left hand glides down.
4. The next step is to begin heeling in circles and then helping your dog sit.
5. Once your dog no longer needs your hand to guide him, the next step is to attach the "Sit" command to his action.

Figure 4.17 Encourage your dog to sit by holding a piece of food in your left hand and slowly moving it backward over his head. He will watch the hand holding the food closely and will sit in order to follow its movement over his head.

The progression is (1) help, command, click, reward; (2) command, help if necessary, click, reward.
6. When your Lab understands the command and can quickly assume the right position, you can change the reward from food to a ball or a tug. The ball or tug will sometimes improve your Lab's focus on you.
7. When your dog understands what Sit requires, slowly remove any extra help you have been giving him until all you need to do is utter the command.

TRAINING SIT AND STAY

The next step is to teach your Labrador Retriever to Sit and Stay. If you have laid a solid Sit foundation, your dog should have no trouble learning to Sit and Stay.
1. When practicing the Sit exercise while walking, give the command to "Sit," and then turn to stand in front of him. If he remains sitting, wait a few seconds and then give the cue word and a reward.
2. Progress to giving the command to "Stay," then taking a step away from him and turning around. Gradually increase the number of steps you take away from the dog.

As always, move forward with training in small steps. When you are walking away, your Labrador Retriever must sit calmly in place.

TRAINING THE DOWN POSITION

Here we have two possibilities for training.

METHOD 1
1. With your Lab siting, hold a treat in front of his nose.
2. Move the treat quickly to the ground between the dog's front legs and hold it there with the palm of your hand facing down.
3. Wait patiently for your dog to lie down. You might slowly pull the treat away from the dog's front legs to make it a little easier for him, as he will then reach forward with his nose.
4. To make sure his whole body touches the ground, slowly move the treat back towards his chest again.

METHOD 2

The following method makes use of two contact points on your dog's body: one at the withers between the shoulder blades and the other at the croup between the hips.

1. Press gently on the withers and croup and give the command "Down." Your Labrador Retriever will lie down.

Figure 4.18 To train the Down position, press gently on two contact points on your dog's body: one at the withers between the shoulder blades and the other at the croup between the hips.

2. Keep your hand on his back when he is down and then give him a food reward.
3. If this goes well, begin waiting until he makes eye contact with you before you give him the treat.
4. After that, give him the reward the moment his body touches the ground.
5. When your Lab understands what is expected when you say "Down" and can assume the position without help, you can begin working at the training center with its distractions. The dog should still go down quickly, lying straight and calm.

6. As soon as he is down, reward him with food.
7. As you have done with other commands, repeat the exercise many times until you know the dog will reliably go down on command.
8. The next step is to combine Down with Stay. Give the command "Stay" and walk backward, away from your dog while facing him. As you move backward, say "Down" and give the reward if he drops to ground.
9. The next progression is to combine Down with heeling. Walk a few paces with the dog and then give the command "Down." Give the reward only if he goes down perfectly. If he does not go down quickly, there is no reward and you should repeat the exercise.
10. Finally, when your Labrador Retriever can heel at a normal speed and go down well, switch up the heeling speeds from

Figure 4.19 Brownie, the chocolate Labrador Retriever puppy, already knows the Down exercise.

Figure 4.20 Young Labrador Retriever Luksi gets a reward for his fast Down.

slow to fast to normal, giving the command "Down" at a variety of paces.

TRAINING THE STAND POSITION
1. Put your dog on a leash and have him Stay with his forelegs parallel to one another. If his legs are slightly out of line, put your hand lightly under your dog's breast to help him stand with his front legs in line. You could put a board or other marker on the ground to help you keep the legs in line.
2. As soon as the position looks good, give your Labrador Retriever a cue word or click and then the reward. Once he understands the position you expect from him, but his Stand is not quite right, allow him to correct himself before giving the reward.
3. As soon as everything is going well consistently, add the command "Stand" to his action. When he is able to Stand at your command without having to correct himself, you can move on to the next step: adding movement.
4. Begin by walking in a circle with your dog heeling on a leash. Only advance a few paces at first before saying "Stand," using your hands, if necessary, to help your dog assume the position

(one hand in front of the nose or on his chest and another under his belly). If all goes well, say the cue word and offer the reward.

5. Progress from this point by working on the position at the training center, which provides all kinds of distractions for your dog. Begin variations by walking backward, facing your dog, before giving the command.

6. Next, train your Labrador Retriever to Stand while you are walking together (the dog at heel) at a variety of speeds: slow, fast, and normal tempo.

Figure 4.21 The Stand exercise is somewhat new for this Labrador Retriever puppy.

TRAINING THE LABRADOR RETRIEVER 123

Figure 4.22 If his legs are slightly out of line for the Stand position, put your hand lightly under your dog's breast to help him stand with his front legs in line. You could put a marker on the ground to help you keep those legs in line.

Figure 4.23 Controlling the dog, especially in a hunting field, is the most important part of training, as this 10-month-old dog shows by following the command "Stay."

Figure 4.24 It is always a delight to see well-trained dogs. These six Labrador Retrievers belong to a gamekeeper we met in Upton Country Park, in England. He came over to talk to me about my camera and told his dogs to sit and wait while we chatted. They were beautifully behaved. When he called them individually by name, they came over one at a time to say "hello" to me and then went back to sit again. They all walked to heel in single file too.

5

The Labrador Retriever as Hunting Dog

In Europe, "bird dogs" had long been used to assist hunters in finding and retrieving game, usually birds. Royalty and other wealthy people used two types of bird dogs for hunting, one for hunting with a falcon and one for hunting with nets. The task of the bird dog during a falconry hunt was to search for and uproot the game. Once the game took flight, falcons could fly up from the hunter's leather glove to "hit" the game. Then the falcons returned to the hunter's arm with the prey. For hunting with nets, the dog had to find the game and lie down in front of it. A net could then be pulled over both dog and game. Bird dogs were generally pointing breeds such as setters, pointers, and spaniels. Pointing breeds hunt with a high nose to capture the smell of the game and point to it.

In the Middle Ages, the invention of firearms greatly increased the effectiveness of hunting. Shotguns allowed people to shoot game at a greater distance. However, when game is shot from a long distance, it is often hit, but not killed. This gives the wounded game the chance to find shelter. Hunters began training their dogs to retrieve: to find the shot or wounded game and bring it back to the hunter. For this, the hunter needed dogs with a good nose, a good memory, a great intelligence, strong conditioning, and enthusiasm.

However, when pointers, setters, and spaniels were trained to retrieve, hunters found they did not point with the same certainty

Figure 5.1 Ben of Hyde, the first registered yellow Labrador, retrieving trout. Ben was born in 1899 at the kennel of Major C. J. Radclyffe.

that they had when it was their sole job. In addition, pointers did not like to go into cold water. For retrieval training, English hunters turned to the poodle and the Labrador as excellent retrievers and swimmers.

CHAMPION RETRIEVERS

An interesting article from *Country Life* magazine about the Retriever Championship Trials in 1910 describes the growing popularity of the Labrador as a hunting dog and also shows how well they performed their duties during the hunting tests:

> One of the signs of the times which the meeting attested is the ever-growing popularity of the Labrador dogs at the expense of the older Curly-Coated Retrievers, which were the friends of our youth; and however sentimental attachment may incline us to be faithful to those old and trusted friends, there is no denying the capabilities of the Labradors, nor, in particular, the energy and pace at which they do their work. It is speed, too, which is achieved without loss of accuracy or care; nor do we find that these high-spirited and vigorous dogs are at all necessarily deficient in the qualities of obedience and control which are so essential in a good retriever.

THE LABRADOR RETRIEVER AS HUNTING DOG

As regards their appearance, we may confess to a personal predilection for our older friends, but that is admittedly a mere question of taste, and so long as the admirers of the looks of the Labradors permit us to preserve our own taste in that respect, we have no ground whatever on which to quarrel with them about theirs.

The entry-list, of nine in all, was not very splendid, but there was some good quality. It was not actually raining when a start was made

Figure 5.2 Over the plough during the 1910 Retriever Championship Trials.

Figure 5.3 Captain Dutton's Labrador Sherborne Togi brings a pheasant to hand.

on the first day, but the rain came down very soon and continued in earnest. The guns were Mr. Glen Kidston himself, Captain de Winton, Captain Harcourt Wood, Colonel Kennedy, Mr. R. Page, Mr. W. Bailey and Mr. Smith Marriott. The withdrawal of Meern, a Flat-Coated Retriever, left the field of eight entirely composed of Labradors.

Peter of Faskally, Mr. Butter's entry, Juniper, Logun Lorna, Sherborne Togi and Kaal were put into a first lot for trials, the judges being Mr. W. Arkwright, Captain H. Eley and Mr. E. G. Wheeler. The dogs, on the whole, brought the game well to hand, while birds were killed out of roots, and Juniper especially did some fast work in very good style. She and Peter of Faskally had the best chances of distinguishing themselves in this first assay and did not miss them. The rest performed uneventful work without any conspicuous failure. In the park, which was the next beat, Logun Lorna and Dock each had a chance to show what was in them, and both retrieved their runners well; but the shooting was a little too deadly to show what many of the dogs could do with wounded birds.

Then came luncheon and therewith a break in the rain, and afterwards the park was taken again, and in that beat Hunsdon Zulu did a fast retrieval of a strong runner, which certainly put him high in the estimation of the judges. A fine task was achieved by Katya here — a pheasant being dropped a long way off, and running into covert [after hiding in shrubbery] was retrieved by her after a brief and fast quest.

Peter of Faskally showed rather an evil disposition to mouth a rabbit in this bout and a disinclination to give the rabbit up kindly. Therewith the first day ended and no dog had the disgrace of being told that its attendance was not needed on the morrow. Therefore all eight reappeared. So also did the sun, and all was warm and beautiful. Kaal and Dock were the first two to be dismissed from the possible champions list, for failure to execute their appointed tasks. On the other hand, Hunsdon Zulu further established his reputation by retrieving one of their little mistakes, and Juniper put in some good work which he just failed to make quite good and complete enough.

The most interesting trial of all was when the guns stood with their backs to the river Llynfi, which was running in flood, while the birds were driven out, some of them pretty high, over their heads. The rocketers fell far back across the stream, and this was the occasion for some very good finding and retrieving. It was indeed remarkable how boldly all the dogs faced the formidable current, hunting their birds well on the far side of it and making their way back with the quarry.

All were good here, but no doubt the judges were very right in their decision to make Mr. Andrew Buxton's Hunsdon Zulu the champion dog, for as far as could be seen he made no mistake in any of the trials that were given him, and in some of the tests he showed up very finely.

Figure 5.4 Winner of the 1910 Retriever Championship Trials was Mr. A. R. Buxton's Labrador, Hunsdon Zulu.

Figure 5.5 Second place was given to Captain Kidston's Labrador, Juniper.

Figure 5.6 Third place was for Major Phillips's Labrador, Katya.

Figure 5.7 Fourth place went to Mr. Butter's Peter of Faskally.

Others might be as brilliant, but none so faultless. Second place was given to Mr. Kidston's Juniper, third to Major Phillips's Katya, and fourth to Mr. Butter's Peter of Faskally.

It was rather unfortunate that more of the winners of the preliminary field trials did not put in an appearance for this championship, but the quality of the champion is not to be denied, and the general standard of the retrieving was high.[1]

Working Dogs

Today, Labradors are still a great help for the hunter as retrievers and are still used in professional hunting, in *battues*, and in hunts on foot. Labrador Retrievers are also particularly suitable for hunting competitions and field trials. They work thoroughly and quickly, paying attention to their surroundings and having an excellent nose. Moreover, they are intelligent dogs that fetch well.

A POLITICAL RETRIEVER

This story from the 1920s presents an amusing anecdote about one dog's ability to distinguish what he has to retrieve:

"Dog stories are just now plentiful in the papers," wrote a correspondent of *The Gentlewoman's Magazine*. My father-in-law once owned a dog that was something of a politician. She was a fine retriever, with a handsome pedigree behind her. The stable-boy had to go every morning to the station for the newspaper, and so this intelligent boy trained the dog to go instead of him every morning, in order that he might indulge in half an hour's longer sleep. "Mat" never failed to bring the paper back on time, but one day she appeared without it, and the stable-boy, [when] hurrying to inquire the reason, [was told by the station-master] that he was short of the *Times* newspaper and had presented a *Telegraph** to the dog instead, who would have nothing to do with it, but laid it down on the floor and came home without. The boy told his master, who naturally was disinclined to believe this story.

The station-master, however, assured him it was true, and, to prove it, a week later my father-in-law rose betimes and hid himself in the station. Sure enough the dog arrived, and on being presented with a *Telegraph*, laid it down on the floor and protested by barking. Then the station-master gave him a *Times*, and the dog trotted off with his parcel. He supposed that the reason was that the paper was of a different weight, and that the ink or paper tasted wrong to the sagacious animal. "Mat" continued to fetch our daily paper for some years, and she even tried to teach one of her sons, with some success, but I regret to say that after her death her son could not be depended on.[2]

---

* *Times* readers are, for the most part, supporters of England's Labour Party, while *Telegraph* readers are supporters of the Conservative Party.

As a working dog, the retriever has the special task of finding shot or wounded game and bringing it back to the hunter. Until called upon to do this task, he must remain stationary next to the hunter and pay particular attention to where the game falls after the shot. The dog must remember (mark) the location where the falling game reached the ground and make a mental map of the location. Marking ability is an important attribute in any retriever. But only after a sign or command from the hunter can the dog search for and retrieve the game. He must also have a "soft mouth" so he does not damage the game by his bite.

Figure 5.8 *The Labrador Retriever Pacha de la Hutte Sauvage in the park of the French town Sauvagère* (1997), by the Belgium artist Albert de Muyser.

During his work, the dog must remain in contact with the hunter so the hunter can send him in the right direction. Upon the hunter's hand gesture or whistle, the dog must stop and immediately sit down. Then the hunter can send the dog to the left, right, or forward with a hand gesture or whistle signal.

But a Labrador Retriever must also be able to work independently and find the shot game in the field, forest, or water through a systematic and persistent search. For this he must have a pronounced search and bring drive, a good nose, and especially the will to find the game.

Retrieving

Let us first take a closer look at the "bring drive" of the Labrador Retriever, which is expressed in retrieving. In the wolf, the ancestor of all dogs, the bring drive is expressed, under the influence of the pack drive, by the animal picking up prey or parts of it and bringing that prey to the lair, where the mother and young pups are waiting.

Figure 5.9 Labrador Retriever Blue Dun von Straßburg-Kärnten (Austria) retrieving a thrown dummy.

The hunting drive and the search and bring drives form a chain that takes care of acquiring food for dogs living in the wild. For pet dogs, which don't need to acquire food, these drives can show up independently. Then we see, for example, that the hunting drive can be present without game and poultry or that the bring drive has nothing to do with food.

The dog's hunting drive and bring drives can be satisfied by replacing prey with a toy, a ball, or a dummy. With some focused training, the dog can be trained to pick up and bring replacement prey.

TEACHING FETCH

If game needs to be retrieved, the dog must go to the area of the fall as quickly as possible. To train for this, find an area with a lawn that has been mowed quite short. Remove a dummy from your hunting bag, and make the dog excited by showing the dummy and moving it around quickly without throwing it. Push the dog a bit away so he comes back to you, then after some time hold your dog and throw the dummy between 3 and 20 feet (1 and 6 m) away. Hold the dog for a moment (to prevent breaking or unsteadiness). Then say the dog's name and give the command "Fetch." Because the dog is already quite excited, he will run straight to the dummy.

TEACHING THE RETURN

You want the dog to quickly pick up the dummy and come back to you. To develop this urge in the dog, stand near a forest edge, corn field, or another training location where you can hide. At the moment the dog reaches the dummy, run out of sight with a loud call. This makes the dog want to return to you as quickly as possible. Because you disappear from sight, the dog won't delay: he will quickly pick up the dummy and come after you. Once the dog is close behind you, turn around, go to your knees, and let him come quickly to you. Do not immediately grab the dummy, but keep the dog with you and reward him. Stay on your knees so you do not hang over the dog, because this can be dominant and threatening. After some time, give the command "Out" and take the dummy. The dog can be presented with a treat so he releases the dummy himself to take the treat.

TEACHING HOW TO HOLD THE DUMMY

When retrieving, the dog can hold the dummy in various ways. Some dogs will hold the dummy at one end, like a cigar dangling from the mouth. However, the dummy is best balanced if the dog holds it in the middle. To teach a dog to do this, use a three-piece dummy. This consists of a heavy middle section with a lighter section attached on both sides. The total weight of this triplet dummy is about 7.7 pounds (3.5 kg). The first time you use this kind of dummy, the dog may look at it strangely. After some encouragement, he will usually pick up one of the outer dummies. But when he tries to bring the dummy back, the other two dummies will drag on the ground. The dog may even step on the dragging dummies, pulling it out of his mouth.

Let the dog solve this problem himself with as little help from you as possible. Eventually the dog will discover that the best place to hold and carry the dummy is by the middle section. He will feel that everything is in balance. It's important to teach a

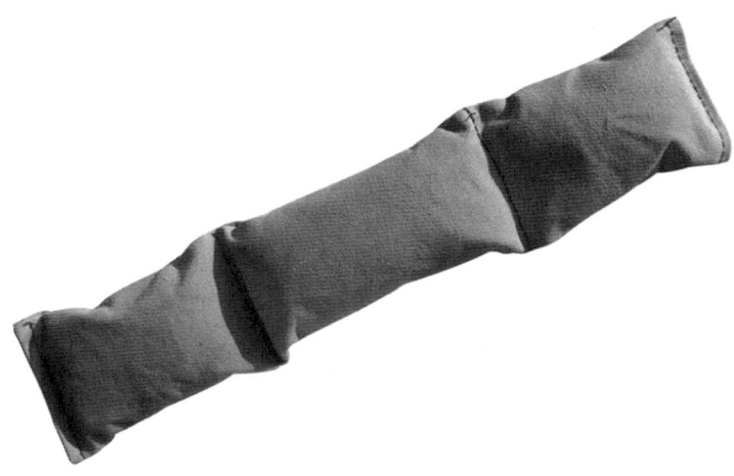

Figure 5.10 A three-piece dummy has a heavy middle section with lighter sections attached on either end.

proper hold in case the dog ever has to carry something like a large hare.

Steadiness

Steadiness means being calm, balanced, solid, and steadfast. Translated to the hunting dog, it means a dog should be calm and attentive and should not demand the hunter's attention. Two forms of steadiness are required: one while sitting next to the hunter and one while walking beside the hunter. When a dog, without command, decides to leave the hunter's side, that is called *breaking* or *unsteadiness*, which is an elimination error in competitions.

If a dog is not steady, you will never be able to show in a trial or competition what great qualities the dog has. An unsteady dog demands too much attention from the hunter. When a dummy is thrown somewhere, and the dog does not see anything because he was focusing elsewhere, the hunter will not have seen anything either, because the dog had his attention. Poor steadiness in a dog is usually caused by poor training buildup by the trainer.

TRAINING STEADINESS

To train steadiness, use a hunting bag with a dummy in it. Go to a quiet area and have the dog sit next to you. Give the dog a command to stay in place, and turn 180 degrees so that you are facing him. Take one step backwards. If necessary, use a hand gesture to tell the dog to wait. After a moment, take the dummy out of the bag. If the dog stays sitting, put the dummy back in the bag, and immediately move to your dog and reward him.

If the dog moves out of place when you take the dummy out, immediately put the dummy back in the bag and say a firm "No!" As soon as he sees the dummy, the dog wants to get it. If he breaks, that urge was stronger than our "Wait" or "Stay" command. But because we still had the dummy in our hand, the dog could not satisfy his urge. His behavior was unsuccessful. Behavior that is unsuccessful will eventually be dropped. Over time, the dog will learn that he better stay sitting. It is important to watch the dog closely to give your "No!" at the right moment.

If the dog consistently remains in place when he sees the dummy, go to the next step. Now stand in front of him and walk backwards about 15 feet (5 m). Take the dummy out of your hunting bag and throw it close in front of you. The flop of the dummy on the ground is enough reason for some dogs to break. If he does, quickly pick up the dummy so the dog doesn't get it. If you notice any moment that the dog wants to move from his place, immediately say "No!" while picking up the dummy. If the dog is still sitting in place by the plop, immediately reward him. Next throw the dummy a few feet to the left or to the right. If the dog goes wrong in this exercise, start training again from the beginning. Don't progress too fast in the training because steadiness is one of the most important skills of a good retriever.

If the dog is properly steady at this point, and you can throw the dummy left or right at your side, you are ready for the next exercise. Stand a few yards in front of the dog. In the hunting bag, in addition to the dummy, have a piece of long grass, folded in half and twisted together. Grab the dummy out of the bag so it is clearly visible for the dog. With your other hand, throw the piece of grass about a yard away from the dog. If the dog is unsteady and breaks, he still won't have success because the piece of grass will fall apart. If you had thrown the dummy instead of the grass, and the dog was unsteady, he would get the dummy before you could grab it. Prevent your dog from having a successful break at all times.

Marking

In hunting, *marking* means a dog seeing and remembering where a bird or dummy has fallen so it can be retrieved when the dog is released to do so. Some hunters use the command "Mark" in order to warn their dogs that something's about to fall or be shot, so they pay attention.

Sometimes the dog can be sent to retrieve immediately, but other times he will have to wait. With a wait, the memory of the dog, but also of the hunter, is put to the test, especially if, in the meantime, more birds or dummies fall and are retrieved by other dogs.

If you do the mark exercise on short grass, your Labrador Retriever will have no trouble marking prey, even at distances of 130 feet (40 m). But in a pasture with tall grass (12 in. [30 cm]), the task becomes more difficult. A good retriever will be able to mark several dummies at once. With the right training, the dog can learn which dummy is first and which one is last to be retrieved. That is why it is so important that a hunting Labrador Retriever learns to focus well when something falls and to remember the area of the fall. That is, it must learn to mark correctly.

TEACHING FOCUS

If you want to teach your dog to focus on a dummy, the moment the dummy flies through the air is very important for the mark. However, if a dark-colored dummy is viewed against a dark background such as group of trees, the dog will have trouble seeing it. A light-colored dummy thrown against a clear sky is also difficult to see. That is why it is good to start with a two-colored dummy that is white on one side and black on the other. Alternatively, you can attach two wide ribbons, one black and one white, to the ends of your dummy. For the first exercises, choose a light dummy that will stay in the air for longer than a heavier dummy. This gives your dog more time to focus on it. If you've attached ribbons to the dummy, it may also make a sound as it moves through the air, further drawing the dog's attention.

A dummy launcher is a handy tool for later mark training. Depending on the type of launcher and dummy, the launch distance can be more than 300 feet (100 m).

In practical gun dog training, eventually the dog must retrieve game instead of a dummy. To train the dog for game, first make a dummy with some feathers or wings of a pheasant or duck. A hunter may be able to provide you with these items. Let the wings dry well first, and then tie them firmly around the dummy. When you want to start using the "wing dummy," work a couple of times with an ordinary dummy, then introduce the wing dummy to your dog.

If the dog quickly retrieves the wing dummy, you can switch to real wild game. People usually use cold dead game for this

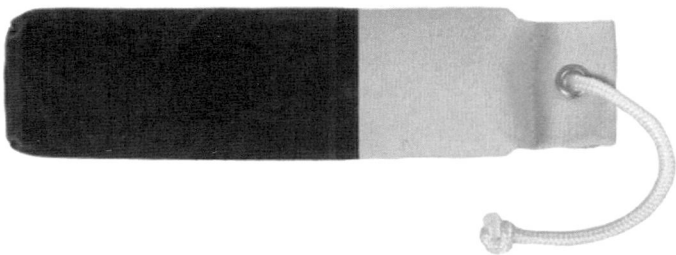

Figure 5.11 The two-colored dummy, white on the top and black on the bottom, can be seen by the dog against every background.

Figure 5.12 A dummy launcher is a handy tool for mark training.

Figure 5.13 A fast return in retrieving a dummy.

stage. Do not use wood pigeons (*Columba palumbus*) for the first training games. This type of bird quickly releases many feathers that can remain in the dog's mouth. This can be unpleasant, making the dog dislike retrieving birds. To prevent this kind of feather loss, you can put a nylon stocking around the pigeon.

Foam dummies can also be used in training. These dummies are made of a soft foam in the shape of a game bird with

Figure 5.14 For the transition from training with a dummy to real game, tie some feathers or wings of a pheasant or duck to the dummy.

Figure 5.15 A hunting Labrador retrieving a bird.

free-swinging, hard plastic feet and a head. Foam dummies stay afloat and have a natural, dead-bird weight. When using a foam dummy, it is advisable to tie wings on them right away, because if you want to go further in gun dog competitions and field trials, you will have to deal with simulated hunting situations, and simulated duck hunts often use plastic lures floating in the water. If a foam duck is tossed between the plastic lures, the dog may have trouble. To his sense of smell, the lures and foam duck smell pretty much the same; they are both made of plastic. We humans live mainly in a visual world, and in the foam duck we see the shape of a duck; to us, this is clearly the target. The dog lives largely in a smelling world and only smells plastic. It may be incomprehensible to the dog why he is not rewarded or is even punished for retrieving the lure but not the foam duck. Sometimes it is the simplest things that make a dog go wrong. In our experience, it's often humans that cause the mistakes dogs make!

However, by tying a pair of real duck wings to the foam duck, everything becomes clear for the dog again. He learns to distinguish the foam duck from the plastic lures and is successful once again.

Figure 5.16 A hunting Labrador retrieving a duck from water.

Figure 5.17 A Labrador Retriever hunting duck.

6

Other Training Possibilities for the Labrador Retriever

Many of the same qualities that make the Labrador Retriever an excellent hunting dog make it appropriate for a wide variety of other working dog roles. For example, because the breed is highly social, eager to learn, intelligent, and human-oriented, they make excellent service and therapy dogs. Their keen sense of smell and desire to work with people also make them excellent detector dogs for a wide and growing list of substances. In this chapter we'll take a brief look at some of the many working dog roles the Labrador plays today.

Service, Therapy, and Facility Dogs

Service dog is the internationally established term for a dog that provides assistance to a person with disabilities and is task-trained to help mitigate the handler's disability. In some countries, the term *assistance dog* may be used synonymously with *service dog*.

Therapy dogs are trained to provide affection and comfort in therapeutic situations. A therapy dog is not the same as a service dog, and therapy dogs don't always have the same rights for public access that service dogs have. A service dog, such as a guide dog, works only with one person and is trained for the person's specific needs. A therapy dog works with numerous people in a variety of situations. Its obedience training allows it to safely provide affection and comfort to people in hospitals, nursing homes, health-care and mental-health facilities, schools, and other locations. The owner is usually the person who visits with the dog. Therapy dogs can assist with physical or occupational therapy, or simply can help calm a patient undergoing a stressful medical procedure.

Figure 6.1 A service dog in training rests after a long day of work.

Facility dogs are often mistakenly called therapy dogs because both may aid people in similar settings, such as health-care environments; however, facility dogs are trained by canine professionals from accredited service dog organizations. The dogs must pass rigorous tests before graduating. Therapy dogs undergo a much less rigorous training process by their owners and are also handled by them. Facility dogs are handled by a wide variety of working professionals, such as physical therapists, psychologists, and special education teachers.

Within the broad areas of service and therapy are many specialties.

Figure 6.2 A naval officer pets Joe, a therapy dog, at a wounded warrior barracks in Afghanistan.

Figure 6.3 A marine enjoys a lighthearted moment with Kea, a service dog with the Hawaii Fi Do during a dog training session. Every Friday, the marines learn how to train dogs from Fi Do, which becomes a form of therapy for marines who are rehabilitating from physical or mental scars as a result of their deployments.

MOBILITY ASSISTANCE DOGS

Mobility service dogs assist people who have mobility issues, such as requiring a wheelchair or having poor balance. The dogs can assist with many general daily activities, such as opening and closing doors, operating light switches and elevator buttons, picking up and carrying objects, or providing balance and stability.

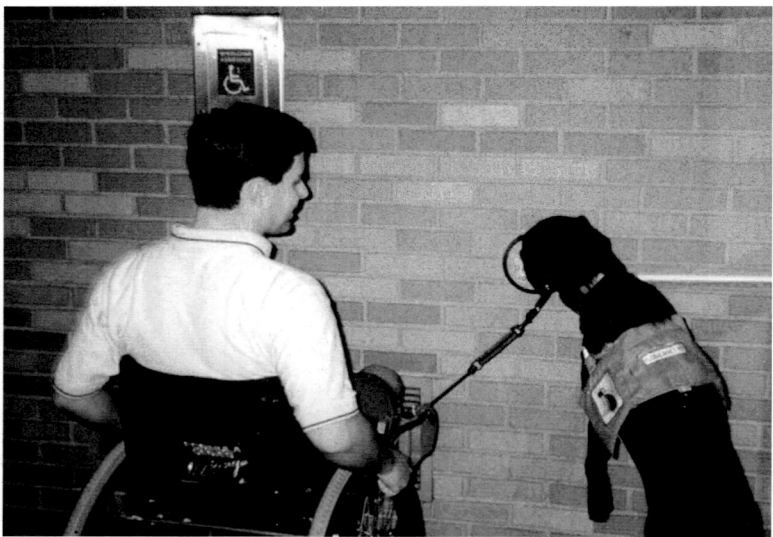

Figure 6.4 Emmet was trained to open a power-assisted door by pushing the wall switch with his nose or his paws.

MEDICAL RESPONSE DOGS

Medical response dogs assist people who have certain types of medical conditions, such as diabetes or epilepsy, by physically alerting to conditions such as an oncoming seizure or a sudden change in blood sugar levels. Medical response dogs are also often trained to help when their handler shows symptoms, such as bringing medications or a telephone, providing bracing and other mobility assistance, or any other number of tasks.

PSYCHIATRIC SERVICE DOGS

Psychiatric service dogs assist a person who has a psychiatric or mental disability, such as autism, post-traumatic stress disorder

Figure 6.5 Mobility service dog training generally starts when the dog is about one year old and lasts four to six months. Mobility service animals may learn up to 70 basic commands.

(PTSD), depression, anxiety, or bipolar disorder. The dogs provide a safe presence that grounds them, but like all service dogs, a psychiatric service dog is individually trained to do work or perform tasks that mitigate a handler's unique disability. Training to mitigate a psychiatric disability may include providing environmental assessment (in cases of paranoia or hallucinations), signaling (such as interrupting repetitive or injurious behaviors), reminding the handler to take medication, retrieving objects, guiding the handler from stressful situations, or acting as a brace if the handler becomes dizzy.

Psychiatric service dogs can also provide companionship for people whose disabilities can make social interactions

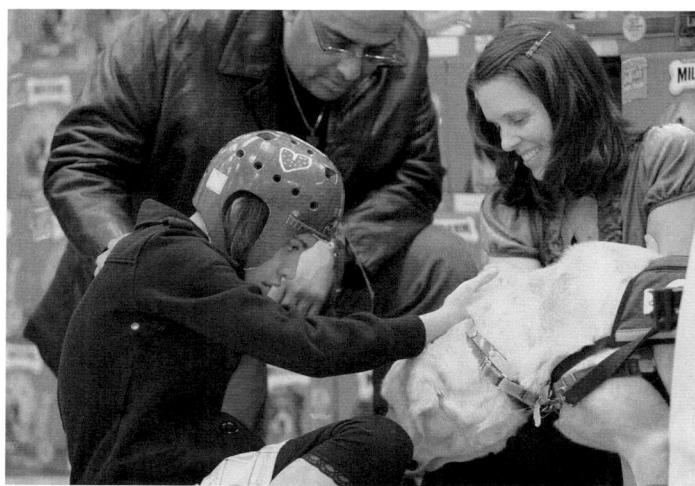

Figure 6.6 A woman with epilepsy meets Carmen during a donation ceremony. How dogs detect an oncoming seizure is unknown. Some researchers believe it develops from a close bond between boss and dog, and that dogs detect subtle changes in human behavior or scent before a seizure occurs.

Figure 6.7 Veterans suffering from PTSD report significantly fewer symptoms and better scores for psychological well-being, coping skills, and other measures of well-being when they have a service dog. PTSD dogs are trained to perform specific jobs, such as averting panic attacks, waking patients from nightmares, creating personal space comfort zones in public situations, and reminding patients to take their medications.

Figure 6.8 A PTSD dog helps get people out of their isolation, so they can take part in social life again. The character of the dog must be in line with the character of the owner — there should be a "click" of connection between the two.

challenging. Children with autism spectrum disorder (ASD) often have problems with anxiety, stress, and mood swings. The autism service dog has been specially trained to support these children. Some autism service dogs are trained to recognize and gently interrupt self-harming behaviors or to help de-escalate an emotional meltdown. For instance, the dog might respond to signs of anxiety or agitation with a calming action such as leaning against the child (or adult) or gently lying across their lap.

HEARING DOGS

Hearing dogs, or signal dogs, assist people with auditory disabilities by alerting the owner to important sounds in the environment, such as doorbells, smoke alarms, alarm clocks, keys

Figure 6.9 A mother walks an autism service dog, with the child tethered to the dog. One study showed that owning a pet dog reduces stress and significantly improves functioning in families who have a child with ASD.

dropping, traffic approaching, or someone calling the person's name. The dog acts as the owner's ears.

The hearing dog can signal in different ways. Tapping with the nose or leg, jumping up, or stopping the owner are possible alerts. How the dog signals depends in part on the dog and the wishes of the boss. Hearing dogs learn both single and double signaling. With single signaling, the dog makes the owner aware of a sound and stays with them. When, for example, the alarm goes off, the dog wakes his owner and stays with them. With double signaling, the dog warns his owner of a sound. When the owner asks the dog "Where?" the dog then leads them to the

Figure 6.10 A therapy dog can help a child learn to self-soothe. Labradors are suitable for use as autism service dogs due to their gentle, reliable character. However, children with autism can sometimes be busy and play rough with the dog, so it is important that the dog can handle this. The dog must always keep calm and radiate stability to the child.

source of the sound, such as a doorbell, the microwave, or a crying baby.

GUIDE DOGS

Guide dogs assist a blind or visually impaired person by leading around or through obstacles, or helping them safely cross the street or stop at curbs. Guide dogs respond to and understand directional commands such as "Forward," "Left," "Right," "Straight on," "Find the stairs," "Find the door," and "Stop." The main task of the guide dog is to help his owner travel from one place to another. In order to guarantee safety, the dog is taught during training to behave as if he is two meters high and one meter wide.

Figure 6.11 A child should never be alone with a dog, but a service dog can be used as a tool for tethering a child with autism who wanders off or bolts. The dog is trained to dig in and resist movement away from the parent.

Service Dog Raising and Training

Puppies with a future as service dogs are usually raised for the first year of life by a host family from the age of seven or eight weeks. The family socializes the pup with other animals, children, city centers, public transportation, and shops and restaurants. The dog must be accustomed to many different kinds of people and situations and be able to handle new situations

OTHER TRAINING POSSIBILITIES FOR THE LABRADOR RETRIEVER

Figure 6.12 Guide dogs can provide people with visual disabilities companionship, independence, and increased confidence in going about day-to-day life.

with calm. The puppies get lots of time to play and cuddle, but also basic training. The pups learn basic commands such as Sit, Down, Stand, Stay, and Come. Obedience is a key aspect of all service dogs. Because young dogs do not always listen perfectly, puppy foster families are well supervised, and they can always go to experienced instructors of the organization with questions and concerns. In short, the family ensures that the dog is healthy, social, and stable when it starts its training.

Once the dog is about one year old, he will be assessed for appropriateness for service work. If he passes, he will begin specialized training for whatever type of service he will enter. A trainer then works with the dog to teach it what it needs to know.

Eventually an owner is matched to the dog, and the customization process begins. Here the dog learns additional commands that are tailored to the situation of the owner. With these additional commands, the dog can help his owner even more. During the final phase of the training, owner and dog learn to work together with a trainer in the owner's home.

Figure 6.13 The task of the dog is to guide his owner safely from one place to another. The dog learns all kinds of commands, but he also learns to ignore some commands if the command can lead to dangerous situations.

An appropriate combination of human and dog is very important. The dog should like to work for his owner, and the owner must be able to handle the dog. Both the dog and human are happiest with a good match. So, for example, a dog with a quick step is preferably connected to someone who likes to walk fast. If an animal has a strong work ethic, he is matched with an owner who is busy and takes on a lot. Ideally there is a click of connection between dog and owner; after this, the two often become inseparable.

Service dogs normally work to an age of about 10 to 12 years. Then they go into a well-deserved retirement, which is ideally with the owner, while the owner starts working with a new dog.

Detector Dogs

The characteristics that make a Labrador Retriever a reliable hunting dog — their keen sense of smell and their desire to interact with people — also make them coveted dogs for detection tasks. Detector dogs must have an exceptional sense of smell, which can flawlessly pick up the smallest clue, as well as a strong search drive, perseverance, concentration, eagerness to learn, and willingness to work with people. All these characteristics are found in the Labrador.

In fact, a 2020 study even showed that the Labrador Retriever may be the superior breed for detection tasks.[1] The study evaluated dog detection performance for narcotics. One of the variables included dog breed: 165 purebred dogs from four breeds were tested. Of these, 46 were German Shepherd Dogs, 41 were Labrador Retrievers, 40 were Malinois, and 38 were Rottweilers. The results demonstrated that Labrador Retriever was the highest in correct alerts and the lowest in false alerts, missed trails, and passes without indication.

It's useful to understand that detector dogs generally have no interest in what they are searching for. Detector dogs use their hunting instinct to search for what they've been *trained* to find. They know that once they've found and alerted for the item their handlers are looking for, they will be rewarded with their favorite toy or a treat. It's a game to the dogs, even though to humans the search may have live and death consequences.

In general, females have a finer sensitivity to odors than males, although their hormonal status before, during, and after they go into heat can affect their interest in work and their odor perception. The same can, of course, be the case with males who smell a female in heat.

Labradors who promise to be successful in nose work are those who make few mistakes while learning a new problem and those who are motivated to perform their task. This high degree of motivation and willingness to complete a task are essential for a detector dog. These qualities can be increased through an effective reward system.

SEARCH AND RESCUE DOGS

Searches for missing people in hard-to-reach areas, as well as for victims under rubble and avalanches, are the most important tasks of search and rescue (SAR) dogs. Labrador Retrievers are very suitable as SAR dogs as long as they are healthy and have no abnormalities in their elbows and hips. The most important characteristics are that the dog likes to work and likes to do assignments with the handler.

Figure 6.14 SAR dogs have saved many lives after natural disasters. Their noses are more efficient at finding human scent than any technology.

HUMAN REMAINS DETECTION

Dogs are also used to detect human remains, or cadavers.[2] In disaster or missing person searches, where a dead body will be the likely outcome of a search action, human remains detection dogs, rather than SAR dogs, are used to search. This is because SAR dogs are trained to find living humans, not decomposing bodies or body parts, which have a different smell.

Human remains detection dogs can locate entire bodies, including those buried or submerged in water; decomposed bodies; body fragments, including blood, tissue, hair, and bones; or skeletal remains. The capabilities of the dog depends on its training. They can also detect residue scents, so they can tell if a body has been somewhere, even if it's not there anymore. Such dogs have clear value for law enforcement when investigating crimes.

DRUG DETECTION DOGS

A drug detection dog is trained to use his senses, mainly smell, to detect a variety of drug substances (e.g., cocaine, heroin, LSD,

Figure 6.15 Cadaver search dogs, here a Belgian police dog, are trained to locate and follow the scent of decomposing human remains, even if the remains have been buried for years and are deep under the surface.

Figure 6.16 Drug detection dogs work wherever people, goods, and mail enter or leave a country, including harbors and international airports. The drug detection dog is the most cost-effective, least invasive, and most visible line of defence in the battle to keep drugs out of workplaces, music festivals, and other big events.

marijuana, methamphetamines, and others). Dogs are trained to locate drug odor sources of varying sizes, from residual amounts to large trafficking quantities. Large amounts of a drug smell different from small amounts, so the dog must be trained to detect various amounts of the same substance as though they are different substances.

EXPLOSIVE AND MINE DETECTION DOGS
Explosive and mine detection dogs save many human lives by warning their handlers of explosive devices. They work with the police and military to locate explosive materials and are trained to detect at least 12 basic odors, which allows them to sense improvised explosive devices (IEDs) and various explosive compositions. Explosive detection is used for cargo inspections and

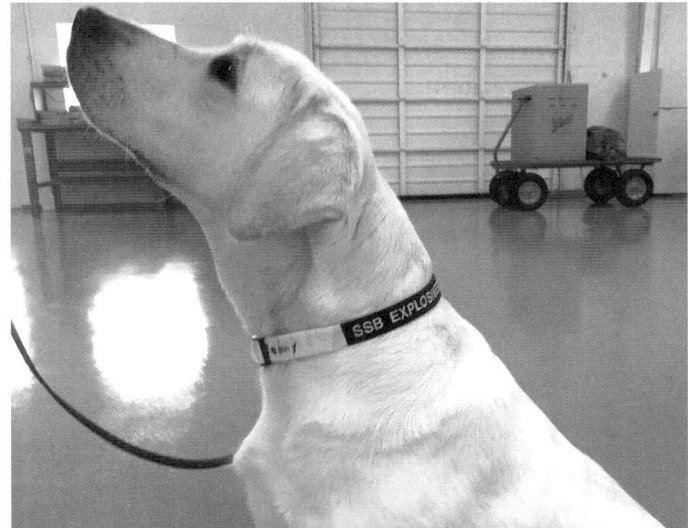

Figure 6.17 The dogs selected by the CIA as explosive and mine detection K9s, mostly Labradors Retrievers, go through a six-week "imprinting" class in which they learn to identify thousands of explosive scents. They are then matched with a Security Protective Service (SPS) K9 handler.

Figure 6.18 A new CIA K9 learning the "Seek" command during the second week of training.

Figure 6.19 The CIA's training facility, set up for a puppy imprinting class.

Figure 6.20 After a dog and CIA handler are matched, the pair undergoes more training, learning to work together as a team to find explosives in locations such as cars, trucks, and luggage.

other preventive searches (bomb checks); searches in response to bomb threats; and specific searches for fireworks, firearms, and/or ammunition.

ACCELERANT DETECTION DOGS

An accelerant detection dog, also called an arson dog, is trained to search quickly and accurately for accelerants that may have been used to start fires. They can find even tiny amounts of accelerants in a scene flooded with several inches of water or covered in snow, ice, mud, or thick layers of debris. Their handlers are law enforcement officers trained to investigate fire scenes.

Figure 6.21 A detective works with 18-month-old Daisy, a Labrador Retriever trained through an insurance company's arson dog program.

MEDICAL DETECTOR DOGS

One of the newest jobs for detector dogs is in medical detection, searching for illnesses such as cancer, COVID-19, malaria, Parkinson's disease, and others. Also called bio-detection dogs, these animals are trained to detect the odor of volatile chemicals that are found in urine, fecal, and skin swab samples from

Figure 6.22 This Labrador Retriever is training to detect the volatile compounds associated with cancer cells. A rotating carousel offers various samples, and the dog reacts to a positive sample by sitting down.

humans with certain specific illnesses. Dogs are not generally trained to detect odors on people directly.

OTHER DETECTING TASKS

It is impossible to include here all the search and detection tasks in which the Labrador Retriever plays an important role. In addition to the jobs noted above, dogs are also employed in the following:

- **Currency detection:** dogs are trained to detect large amounts of concealed money
- **Tobacco detection:** dogs search for illegal tobacco
- **Biosecurity detection:** dogs help protect countries from exotic pests and diseases from agricultural sources
- **Cell phone detection:** dogs in prisons detect phones and items concealed in the phones
- **Ore deposit detection:** dogs are trained to find certain mineral deposits
- **Mold detection:** dogs, sometimes called *rothounds*, search inside buildings for fungi that cause decay and deterioration of timber

Figure 6.23 Mold detection dogs search buildings for fungi that cause buildings to decay. Dogs can pinpoint the location of decay long before it becomes apparent to human eyes.

- Bed bug detection: exterminators and property owners enlist specially trained dogs to find where bed bugs are hiding as well as for follow-up, to determine if an extermination method has worked
- Oil and gas detection: dogs search for leaks in pipelines and valves located above or below ground to avoid costly, hazardous spills and environmental damage

7

Health Care and Caring for the Older Dog

Health care is important for every pet but even more important for the Labrador Retrievers we use as working dogs. A great deal is required of working dogs, both physically and mentally. Working dog handlers must always make the health and safety of their Labrador Retriever a top priority. A Labrador will always go to the extreme of its physical abilities for the handler. That is why we sometimes have to protect these specialists against their own desire for work and give them the rest they need.

In this chapter, we will tell you more about the mental and physical health of your Labrador Retriever and hereditary defects in the breed. We also give advice for how to deal with your working dog as he ages and what your dog can contribute after decertification.

The Healthy Dog

Basic data, such as pulse, respiration, body temperature, and state of hydration or dehydration are important in order to determine your Labrador Retriever's state of health or illness. Sometimes even one of these data can help a veterinarian diagnose a dog's illness. Therefore, it is good to know the basic data of a dog in normal good health.

HEALTH CARE AND CARING FOR THE OLDER DOG

Figure 7.1 Labrador Retrievers as a breed develop late and often do not reach full maturity until they turn at least two years of age.

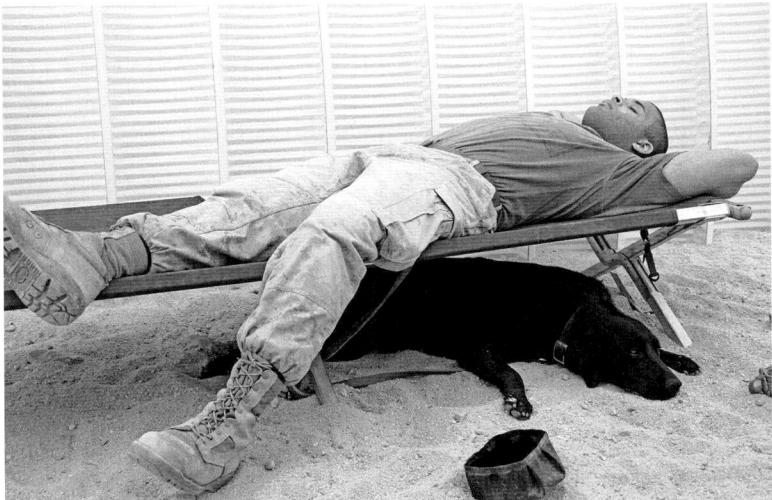

Figure 7.2 A US military dog handler takes a break with his five-year-old black Lab, a specialized search dog.

PULSE

The normal heartbeat of dogs at rest varies according to age:

- **Puppies and very young dogs:**   110–120 beats/minute
- **Adult dogs:**   90–100 beats/minute
- **Older dogs:**   70–80 beats/minute

Of course, the pulse rate increases during exertion.

In order to find your dog's heartbeats per minute, count the pulses for exactly 15 seconds and multiply this number by four. It would be better to count pulses for one minute, but because some dogs are so fidgety, this can be difficult.

The easiest way to find a dog's pulse is to place your hand on the left breast, but this method will not allow you to notice the intensity of the heartbeat. You can also count the pulse by laying your forefinger and middle-finger at the femoral artery on the inside of one of the hind legs, high on the leg, almost at the place where the hind leg ends and the belly begins. Finding this place can be difficult. But if you cannot feel the pulse on the femoral artery of a sick dog, this is a bad sign. A dog's pulse is naturally irregular, so don't worry about that. Also know that an ill dog usually has a faster heartbeat than a healthy dog.

RESPIRATION

Like pulse, breathing frequency differs depending on the age of the dog. The number of breaths per minute and the depth of breathing give an indication of the health of the dog.

- **Young dogs:**   20–22 breaths/minute
- **Adult dogs:**   16–18 breaths/minute
- **Older dogs:**   14–16 breaths/minute

Depending on factors such as age, pregnancy, body weight, and environmental temperature, respiration will fluctuate between 10 and 40 breaths per minute. Of course, the dog's breathing, like its pulse, also increases during exertion. Normally the dog will breathe through mouth and nose, but in excitement, heat, and exertion, the dog will start panting. Panting in rest is usually a sign that the dog feels unwell, although it also occurs after being outside in hot weather. If you want to count the dog's breathing, count only the inhalation or the exhalation, but not both.

TEMPERATURE

The normal body temperature of the adult dog is 100.76°F (38.2°C), with a range between 99.5°F (37.5°C) and 102.2°F (39.0°C). A dog's temperature in the morning and evening can differ between 0.5°C and 1.0°C. In order know whether your dog has a fever, you have to know his average morning and evening temperature on healthy days. A digital thermometer that measures the temperature of the inner ear is useful; it is easy to handle, quick to measure, and less annoying for the dog than other thermometers. If the dog has a fever, measure the temperature several times a day in order to give the vet full information about the situation.

DEHYDRATION TEST

The test for dehydration should be performed first with your healthy dog in order to know the difference between the normal situation and dehydration. For this test, pull the dog's skin up a little at the back of the neck, or better, pull the fold of the skin at the side of the chest. If you let it out, the skin should immediately return to its former position. If the skin remains standing up after letting go, the dog is dehydrated and you need to visit a vet immediately. Table 7.1 gives a clinical estimation of the measure of dehydration in dogs.

Table 7.1. Degree of Dehydration in Dogs

% DEHYDRATION	CLINICAL INVESTIGATION	THERAPY
<5	• No clinical test	Quench thirst
6	• Slight resistance of the skin fold	Administer oral liquid
8	• Some resistance of skin fold • Slight inflammation of the eye • Dry mucous membrane in the mouth	Infusion
10–12	• Severe resistance of skin fold • Obvious inflammation of the eye • Cold extremities – muscular spasms	Infusion
12–15	• Shock: life threatening urgency	Urgent infusion

10 Points for Daily Health Control

The achievements of dogs in operational service have improved greatly over the past few decades. Reasons for this improvement include better training methods and better nutrition. Our dogs now perform better, but much more is also requested of them. The dog handler or owner plays a key role maintaining an animal's health, and before a Labrador Retriever is taken into training or operational service, the handler has to be sure the dog is well prepared and healthy. If it isn't, the dog will become physically exhausted after only a brief exertion. For instance, with poor or insufficient feeding, the dog lacks concentration and energy and shows intense nervousness. Every dog handler should look at the following 10 points daily to see if their dog is healthy enough for training or deployment.

Figure 7.3 A chocolate Labrador Retriever in fine physical form.

1. Movement. When your dog gets up and walks around, watch the way he moves. Be aware of the following warning signs that something is wrong:
- Stiffness
- Difficulty getting up or down
- Unwillingness to walk
- Unusual quietness
- Restlessness

2. Feces and urine. Keep an eye on the regularity of your dog's waste elimination and make sure the feces is consistent.

Indications of concern (feces)
- Diarrhea
- Constipation
- Mucus
- Blood

Indications of concern (urine)
- Darkness
- Cloudiness
- Blood

3. Body check. Check your dog's body for lumps, cuts, inflammation, and any signs of discomfort. Does the coat feel smooth and healthy? Watch for the following signs of concern:
- Lumps
- Flinching
- Moisture

4. Feet and claws. Check the pads of the feet by moving the limbs backward (never to the side). Watch for the following signs of concern:
- Matted fur
- Discharge
- Damage
- Broken nails
- Foreign objects

5. Ears. Feel with your fingers over the pinna (the flappy parts) and the rest of the ear surface. Then look inside the ear canal. A normal ear should be cool, soft, and pale pink. Wax is normal, but the ear should be generally clean and there shouldn't be a bad odor or swelling. Check for the following:

- Lumps or bumps
- Areas of pain
- Moisture
- Unusual discharge

6. Eyes. The dog's eyes should be clear, and there should be no excessive discharge or signs of irritation. Watch for the following:

- Ingrown eyelashes or hair that can touch the eyes
- Eyes that are not equally open
- Pupils that are not the same size
- Squinting
- A dog's need to rub its eyes
- Bulging
- Foreign objects
- Scratches
- Clouding or discoloration

7. Nose. Your dog's nose should be moist and cool. Signs of concern include the following:

- Discharge
- Sneezing
- Uneven or obstructed breathing

8. Mouth and teeth. Check the mouth for anything out of the ordinary. Lift the upper lip to observe the color of the gums just above the upper canine teeth. Healthy gums are usually a bubble-gum or salmon-pink color; however, what is normal can vary from dog to dog. Indications of a problem include the following:

- Darker/redder than normal or pale gums
- Bad breath
- Growths and lumps inside the mouth
- Cuts and sores on the tongue

For a quick check, lift up the mouth flaps and make sure the teeth are clear and that none are loose. Then take a look inside the mouth. Watch for the following:

- Lumps
- Broken/chipped teeth

- Inflamed areas
- Swelling
- Bleeding gums

9. Anus. Dogs have sacs on either side of the anus that fill with fluid produced by the anal glands. This fluid is assumed to be a scent marker useful for delineating territory. Symptoms of problems with the anal sacs include the following:

- Scooting
- Straining to defecate
- Itching/scratching
- Tail chasing
- Discharge from the anal glands
- Licking and biting around the anus

10. Genital area. A healthy dog should have no discharge in the genital area, although a small amount of whitish-yellow smegma can accumulate around the preputial opening and is completely normal. The presence of preputial discharge that includes blood, urine, or pus is more serious and suggests an underlying problem, ranging from a mild, relatively benign disorder to a severe, even life-threatening disease.

Symptoms of concern (males)
- Spotting
- Swelling or inflammation
- Excessive licking
- Discharge
- Lethargy
- Fever
- Lack of appetite

Symptoms of concern (females)
- Discharge from the vulva
- Spotting of blood
- Scooting
- Attracting males
- Frequent urination
- Frequent licking of the vagina

Physical Defects in Labradors

Due to many years of careless breeding, especially for show reasons, the Labrador Retriever has acquired a variety of physical defects. Dogs diagnosed with serious eye or movement defects cannot become working dogs or must be taken out of service. The following conditions are listed as defects (most of them congenital) in the Labrador Retriever:

- **Addison's disease**: hypoadrenocorticism, an inadequate secretion of cortisone from the adrenal glands
- **Allergies**
- **Atopy**: allergy to an inhaled substance
- **Carpal subluxation**: wrist bones that are loose and out of alignment
- **Cataract**: a change in the structure of the lens of the eye, leading to cloudiness and usually blindness
- **Central progressive retinal atrophy** (CPRA): also known as retinal pigment epithelial dystrophy (RPED), or day-blindness. This is a familial disease characterized by the appearance of clumps of pigment in the posterior pole (area centralis) of the fundus. As the pigmented zone advances, the dog may show signs of day-blindness. See also progressive retinal atrophy (PRA), night-blindness.
- **Chronic hepatitis**: the most common liver disease in dogs; can be an inherited defect. Labs are predisposed to copper-associated chronic hepatitis, a defect caused by copper accumulation in the liver.
- **Cold water tail**: also called limber tail syndrome or broken tail, a painful condition in which the tail of the dog hangs down from the tail base or is held horizontally for 3 or 4 inches and then drops down. The condition can occur after swimming, or even after a bath with cold water or water that is too warm. However, it can also happen after a heavy day of work that involves a lot of tail action.
- **Coloboma**: abnormal development of the eye, which can lead to blindness
- **Congenital hypotrichosis**: an abnormally small amount of hair growth

- **Corneal dystrophy**: abnormality of the cornea, usually characterized by shallow pits in the surface
- **Craniomandibular osteopathy**: abnormal development of the bones of the face and the jaw
- **Cystinuria**: abnormal excretion of cystine in the urine
- **Dacrocystitis**: inflammation of the tear sac
- **Deafness**
- **Dentition faults**: abnormal placement, number, or development of teeth
- **Diabetes mellitus**: metabolic disease caused by insulin deficiency
- **Distichiasis**: abnormal eyelashes, which can lead to corneal ulcers, chronic eye pain, excessive tearing, and eyelid spasms
- **Dwarfism**: abnormal growth pattern, resulting in an undersized dog
- **Ectropion**: abnormal rolling out of the eyelids
- **Elbow dysplasia**: abnormal development of the elbow joint
- **Epilepsy**: disease characterized by seizures and/or disturbances of consciousness
- **Epitheliogenesis imperfecta**: a genetic condition in which the hair and epidermis fails to develop on parts of the body
- **Familial reflex myoclonus**: idiopathic disease of skeletal muscle
- **Fragmented coronoid process**: osteochondrosis of the elbow joint
- **Gastric dilatation volvulus (GDV)**: gastric torsion or bloat, caused by a twisting of the stomach that traps the stomach contents and gases, resulting in a rapid swelling of the abdomen accompanied by pain and, if untreated, death
- **Hemophilia A**: factor VIII deficiency, prolonged bleeding episodes
- **Hemophilia B**: factor IX deficiency, prolonged bleeding episodes
- **Hepatic portosystemic shunt**: malformation of blood vessels in the liver

- **Hereditary myopathy**: neuromuscular disease in which the muscle fibers dysfunction, resulting in muscular weakness, muscle cramps, stiffness, or spasms; an autosomal recessive trait in both black and yellow Labs
- **Hip dysplasia** (HD): developmental malformation or subluxation of the hip joints
- **Hot spots**: moist dermatitis, a localized area of a severely itchy, inflamed, and oozing skin exacerbated by the animal's intense licking and chewing at the spot
- **Hypertrophic osteodystrophy**: abnormal inflammation of bones with pain and development of excessive bony growths
- **Hypoglycemia**: abnormally low blood glucose
- **Hypothyroidism**: endocrine disease in which the body produces an abnormally low amount of thyroid hormones
- **Isolated processus anconeus**: a loose part inside the elbow joint
- **Lick dermatitis**: skin disease caused by an animal's excessive licking, especially on the legs and paws
- **Melanoma**: rare cancer developing from the skin cells that produce pigment
- **Muscular dystrophy**: a progressive degeneration of skeletal muscles
- **Narcolepsy**: neurological disorder characterized by falling asleep suddenly, which can occur during periods of activity and last for varying lengths of time
- **Ocular chondrodysplasy**: abnormal cartilage formation of the eye globe and/or socket
- **Osteochondritis dissecans**: specific form of inflammation of the cartilage of certain joints, causing arthritis
- **Osteochondrosis**: developmental disease resulting in abnormal formulation of joint cartilage; commonly involves the shoulder, stifle, hock, or elbow
- **Persistent hyaloid artery**: developmental abnormality where a blood vessel inside the eye does not atrophy as it should
- **Persistent pupillary membrane**: developmental abnormality where the membrane forming the iris does not form properly

- **Progressive retinal atrophy** (PRA): slow deterioration of the retina, producing night-blindness; see central progressive retinal atrophy
- **Prolapsed rectum**: inside of the rectum protrudes outside the anus
- **Prolapsed uterus**: the uterus protrudes into the vaginal canal
- **Retinal dysplasia**: abnormal development of the retina
- **Seborrhea**: skin disease with excess scaling of the skin and often an excess of sebum and odor
- **Shoulder dysplasia**: looseness of the shoulder
- **Strabismus**: condition in which the eyes are not properly aligned with each other
- **Tracheal collapse**: a malformation of the cartilage rings that make up the trachea, giving them the tendency to collapse
- **Tricuspid valve dysplasia** (TVD): malformation of the valve on the right side of the heart, between the right atrium and the right ventricle
- **Von Willebrandt's disease**: bleeding disorder caused by defective blood platelet function

Preventing Physical Strain

Training and operational service place a heavy strain on the Labrador's body. For example, when a dog jumps, not only are the muscles of its hindquarters and back forced to exert themselves, but also the joints, particularly the forepaws, have to cope with a jarring load when it lands.

Intensive searching requires concentrated muscular movements, often employing an unnaturally stretched and bent posture. This causes an extra load on the joints, and the muscle activity produces lactic acid in the muscles.

WARM-UP

To prepare the dog's body for such a performance, warm-up exercises are strongly recommended. Without a warm-up, the risk of acute injuries is very high. Warm-ups primarily help the muscles,

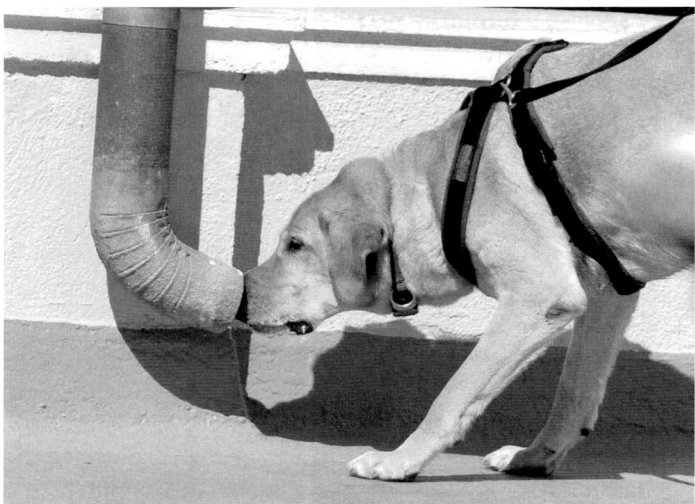

Figure 7.4 Although hunting, and especially retrieving, was the first task the Labrador Retriever undertook for humans, today the breed works in many areas, such as service and detection work.

Figure 7.5 Wayfield's Young Argos, a fox red, English-line Labrador retriever, returns with a duck from a successful pond retrieval.

but they also help prevent injury to the ligaments, tendons, and joints. A safe, effective warm-up consists of three phases.

Phase 1 involves relaxed movement of the body for 2 minutes. This allows the muscles, as well as the heart and vascular system, to slowly activate from rest. This phase can consist of calmly walking with the dog for about 1 minute and then moving on to an easy trot or jog.

This easy trot can be the start of **Phase 2** by increasing the tempo for 2 or 3 minutes into a full trot, increasing the blood circulation. Ensure you trot not only in a straight line, but also in circles. This activates the muscles that permit sideward movements and supplies them with blood. The easiest way to do this is to run with the dog or train it to run beside a bike.

Phase 3 involves strong muscular exertion and active stretching for 1 to 2 minutes. The muscles have to be contracted and stretched actively to be fully prepared for training or active service. Trotting up and down a hill or slope is perfect. The advantage of a hill or slope is that the dog's muscles are stretching at the same time that they are contracting: uphill the hindquarters, downhill the front leg.

COOL DOWN

After training or operational service, do not immediately put your dog in the car or kennel, or play fetching drills with a ball. Instead, lead your Labrador through a cool down, which will help ensure a quick recuperation after a performance. The muscles have to top up their glycogen stock; small damage to the muscles, tendons, and ligaments have to be repaired; and waste products have to leave the muscles and then the dog's body. The most common way to cool down a dog is to go for an easy run. After active service or training, an appropriate cool down consists of 3 minutes of trotting easily, followed by 2 minutes of normal walking. By then, most of the muscles, joints, and ligaments will have had enough circulation to cool down effectively.

Preventing Mental Strain

For normal physical and mental development, every animal needs appropriate stressors that help it adapt to the conditions

Figure 7.6 A US marine and his IED detection dog.

in its environment. The effects of positive stress include optimal preparedness: quick reactions and physical strength and speed because of an increased supply of energy from the body. The effects of negative stress due to chronic or strong stress include diseases of the immune system or kidneys and gastrointestinal or cardiovascular problems. In dogs, negative stress can also result in a high aggressive impulse.

The threshold for physical or mental damage from stress differs from animal to animal and depends on many different variables, such as hereditary factors, state of health, experiences, and severity of the stress. A situation that one dog experiences calmly can for another dog be a heavy burden. There are five main groups of stressors:

1. **External stressors**: inundation with stimuli of the sense organs (e.g., light, noise, odor, heat, cold) or withdrawal of stimuli (deprivation), pain stimuli, and real or simulated dangerous situations
2. **Stressors that prevent the satisfaction of primary needs**: lack of sleep, withdrawal of food or water, no or less-than-normal bodily contact, undue restriction of movement (chaining up or kenneling)

Figure 7.7 An Austrian Red Cross dog handler during disaster training in Budapest, Hungary. After a correct find, his Labrador Retriever got a tennis ball in a sock to play with as a reward.

3. **Performance stressors**: physical overexertion; over- or undertraining; incorrect training methods; excessive demands in training or operational service; inappropriate activity for the breed or dog; tests; anticipation of possible failures, reprimands, or punishment
4. **Social stressors**: isolation, less or no contact with other dogs, incorporation into a new dog group, removal from a dog group, change of human partner

Figure 7.8 Labrador Retrievers are used in a lot of dog sports, such as agility training.

5. **Mental stressors**: conflicts, uncontrollable situations, anxiety, uncertain expectations, inconsistency in the human relationship, noisy surroundings, irregular days, constantly changing environment

SYMPTOMS OF STRESS

Below are some of the symptoms that indicate a dog is stressed — often more than one symptom can be observed at the same time.

Some of these behaviors, such as panting, may also occur when the dog is not stressed at all (maybe it is a hot day or the dog has been playing). However, knowing the symptoms of stress will help you assess your dog's well-being when you know it has faced stressful stimuli.

- **Panting**: While under stress, the dog has a higher pulse rate and muscular tension, for which more oxygen is used. In addition, increased metabolism means the body produces more heat. Both situations can lead to panting.
- **Salivation**: In some dogs, excessive salivation is seen after agitation or stress, often combined with excessive panting.
- **Self-destruction**: This is often seen in the form of excessive licking and biting of the extremities, tail, and/or genital area. These parts of the dog's body eventually become open and painful wounds. In response to pain stimuli, the body releases endorphins, the body's own painkillers, also called the "feel-good" hormones. By controlling pain and giving the feeling of well-being, endorphins are similar to morphine. That feeling of analgesia and well-being helps the dog endure the stressful situation, but it can come to rely upon it, resulting in compulsive, self-destructive behavior.
- **Destruction of objects**: This usually occurs with dogs that are left alone for long periods.
- **Exaggerated bark or whimpering**: Continuous barking, whimpering, and howling can be symptoms of an overloaded and stressed dog.
- **Trembling**: While under stress, the muscles are tensed; by trembling, the body tries to relax the muscles to avoid muscle cramps.
- **Nervousness**: The dog is easily startled and distracted. At events or in situations in which it normally stays quiet and calm, the dog now reacts with restlessness, agitation, anxiousness, or aggression.
- **Diarrhea and enuresis**: During fear or at a sudden fright, the intestinal tract activates, resulting in defecation and increased frequency of urination. Prolonged or excessive stress can cause diarrhea.

- **Lack of appetite**: This is a well-known sign of dogs in stress, often seen in boarding kennels. However, excessive demands in training can also make the dog refuse or spit out food or rewards.
- **Gluttony**: The opposite of the dog refusing to eat in stressful situations is the dog that gorges itself with everything it can find. This sometimes includes inedible objects such as wood, paper, and stones.
- **Lack of concentration**: The dog is distracted and nervous in training or operational service. Well-known situations or exercises seem to be forgotten. The dog may show poor concentration for learning new exercises or in new situations.

We bring our working Labradors, sometimes unknowingly, into difficult and stressful situations. It is important that the handler learns to see what is stressful for the dog, which can, of course, vary depending on the dog's age or state of health. Many things can cause stress: crowds, noise, and traffic just to name a few. Different dogs handle these things better or worse than others. Their ability to cope with stressors comes from various factors, such as genetic predisposition, experiences, and training.

It is important to realize what you are asking from your dog and whether your dog can handle your demands. Consider carefully what you ask of your dog and observe whether your dog can handle it. Make sure you give the dog breaks and enough time for physical and mental recovery.

Caring for Older Labs

With current nutrition and veterinary care standards, it is not uncommon for Labrador Retrievers of 9 and 10 years old to provide excellent performances, both in training and in operational service. When working with older Labs, maintaining their positive attitude and interest is far more challenging than maintaining good physical condition. Attitude can often be improved by added days of rest and extra personal attention. Extra care should be taken to ensure that older Labrador Retrievers are not overweight and that their diet is suited to their age. Some older dogs

Figure 7.9 A US army dog handler and his working dog in Iraq.

may develop mineral or vitamin deficiencies that can be remedied by simple, inexpensive dietary supplements.

Many older dogs develop slight stiffness in their legs and back when they first get up or when they come out of their kennel. Extra care should be taken to limber up these dogs before they start their operational duty, either by massage or through warm-up exercises.

Care should also be taken that in operational service not too much is required of older dogs. Therefore, it is useful to know what happens in the ageing dog. Older dogs react differently to performances than younger dogs do in many ways, and their recuperation is also different. In general, it can be said that the body of an older dog reacts more strongly to stressful situations. Body tissue and cells are more easily upset with heavy loads, and therefore the same load in older Labrador Retrievers will become an overload that would be handled easily by a young dog.

In other words, the moment at which the dog's body reacts to an overload will be sooner as the dog ages. Below we discuss how a dog ages after age 7 and then age 10. Individual dogs will show aging at different rates, but the ages 7 and 10 give a rough approximation of the stages of age-related changes.

In Labrador Retrievers over 7 years old, we can expect a slower recovery from a performance as their muscle mass decreases. Both the slower recovery and decreasing muscle mass are effects of the decreasing number of hormones in the ageing body.

As a dog ages, its organs begin to degenerate. In 70 percent of dogs over 7 years old, renal function has decreased, and 30 percent have heart valve damage. Damage to the organs is partly a natural consequence of the ageing process, in which waste products accumulating in the cells cause the quality of the cells to decline. It is also a consequence of small inflammation processes in the organs, especially in the kidneys and heart valves. A slipped disc in older dogs is often the result of degeneration: the quality of the disc wall decreases, which allows the disc's core to move and press on the nerve or spinal marrow.

As the dog ages, the quality of joint cartilage decreases; it doesn't hold water as well, so its buffering effect decreases. This degeneration of the cartilage leads to damage, which in turn leads to inflammation: the beginning of arthritis. Compounding this, as a result of intensive training over many years, a working Lab's joints have sustained many small injuries. The sum of such micro-traumas also leads to arthritis.

After 10 years of age, the overall degeneration seen in dogs over 7 years of age occurs faster. All the aforementioned processes become more present after age 10 and to a greater extent. Besides degeneration, a number of other organs at this age will not work properly. We can also expect a decrease of the sense of sight when geriatric cataracts arise. The quality of the retina can decrease, and as a result the dog can observe his surroundings less well. After age 10, hearing can also decrease because of abnormal bone growth in the inner ear. Your Lab may respond less well or not at all to given commands.

The Decision to Decertify

When do we have to decertify a Labrador Retriever from operational service? Most of the time that decision is very difficult for the handler or owner. The Lab's health fails gradually, and it is challenging to assess when mental and physical stress have

become too much. However, there are some clear signs that it is time to retire the dog from operational service:
- The dog walks with a slight limp every time after training or operational service.
- Two to three days after training or operational service, the dog is sulky and stiff.
- Without medication (analgesic, inflammation inhibitor), the dog cannot function in a normal way.
- The dog is often startled by unexpected or loud noises, or by strange objects in a familiar situation.

In older Labrador Retrievers, the effects of old age become more noticeable. The degeneration cannot be stopped, but it can be delayed by modifications in operational service and training, a suitable diet, and nutritional supplements. The goal of the

Figure 7.10 The Labrador Retriever has much that appeals to people, such as its gentle ways, intelligence, and adaptability. These make it an ideal dog.

handler should be to continue the dog's useful life for as long as possible.

The decision to decertify a dog from active service is certainly not easy. But as soon as the Lab suffers from training or work more often than not, stopping is best. No matter how difficult the decision to retire a good Labrador Retriever may be, it often turns out that after retirement, if the dog lives as a pet, he revives and lives a good life.

Continue to train your decertified dog in an easy way; in particular, let him use his specialty now and then: go tracking, let him search for the objects he was trained for (drugs, explosives, people, etc.), carefully do obedience exercises, or whatever he likes. Returning the older dog to the training school to act as a training aid for new students is another method of increasing the dog's useful life. The dog can be used by successive classes of students and can be rested when medical problems erupt.

Most importantly, never stop the dog's work completely and suddenly. Besides the Lab's natural working drive, every dog has also an occupational drive. However old the dog may be, it still wants to be useful and be a valuable member of the dog/handler community. Therefore give your dog the opportunity to show you his training until his dying day. Your Labrador Retriever has, of course, deserved that!

Reading List

American Kennel Club. (2019). *Official standard for the Labrador Retriever.* http://images.akc.org/pdf/breeds/standards/LabradorRetriever.pdf

Ash, A. C. (1927). *Dogs: Their history and development.* Houghton Mifflin Co.

Assistance Dogs International. (2021). The global authority in the assistance dogs industry. https://assistancedogsinternational.org

Barker, S. B., & Wolen, A. K. (2008). The benefits of human-companion animal interaction: A review. *Journal of Veterinary Medical Education, 35*, 487–495.

Bergman, P. (2017). *Ore dogs and economic geology: Developments in exploration methods and technologies.* Elsevier.

Boilieu, L. De. (1861). *Recollections of Labrador life.* Saunders, Otley, & Co.

Bomers, M. K., van Agtmael, M. A., Luik, H., Vandenbroucke-Grauls, C. M. J. E., & Smulders, Y. M. (2014). A detection dog to identify patients with *Clostridium difficile* infection during a hospital outbreak. *Journal of Infection, 69*(5), 456–461. https://doi.org/10.1016/j.jinf.2014.05.017

Brisbin, I. L., & Austad, S. N. (1991). Testing the individual odour theory of canine olfaction. *Animal Behaviour* (42), 63–69.

Broadley, G. (1968). *The Retriever owner's encyclopaedia.* Pelham Books.

Bylandt, H. A. van. (1894). *Hondenrassen* (Dog Breeds, Volume 1: Hunting Dogs). Kluwer, Deventer.

Cairns, D. (1911). The Duke of Buccleuch's Labradors at Langholm Lodge. *Country Life,* 2 December.

Cairns, D. (1912). The Hon. A. Holland-Hibbert's Labradors. *Country Life,* 3 August.

Canadian Kennel Club. (2019). *Official breed standards: Labrador Retriever.* https://www.ckc.ca/en/Files/Breed-Standards/Breed-Standards/Group-1-Sporting-Dogs

Cattet, J., & Hardin, D. S. (2014). *Diabetes alert dogs: Buyer beware.* Diabetes Forecast. http://archives.diabetesforecast.org/2014/11-nov/diabetes-alert-dogs-buyer.html

Central Intelligence Agency. (2017). *CIA's top 10 dog training tips.* Central Intelligence Agency. https://www.cia.gov/stories/story/cias-top-10-dog-training-tips/

Champion retrievers. (1910). *Country Life,* 12 November, 694–696.

Church, J., & Williams, H. (2001). Another sniffer dog for the clinic? *Lancet, 358,* 930.

Clarke, B. (1981). *Inuit in Labrador.* The Rooms Provincial Museum website. https://www.therooms.ca/inuit-in-labrador

Coode, C. (1993). *Labrador Retrievers today.* Ringpress Books.

Cormack, W. E. (1873). *Narrative of a journey across the island of Newfoundland.* St. John's, Newfoundland.

Craig, D. (2008). *The Labrador Retriever.* (Best of Breed Series). Magnet & Steel.

Doherty, M. J., & Haltiner, A. M. (2007). Wag the dog: Skepticism on seizure alert canines. *Neurology, 68*(4), 309. doi:10.1212/01.wnl.0000252369.82956.a3

Dominik, D. (2000). Attempts towards determination of influence of scent background upon indications by dogs. Paper presented at conference: Osmology: overestimated or neglected area of forensic science? *Problemy Kryminalistyki,* 230, 56–58.

Edwards, R. (2005). *Sandylands: An historical perspective.* Sandylands.net. http://www.sandylands.net/history2.html

Fédération Cynologique Internationale. (2019). *Labrador Retriever breed standard.* http://www.fci.be/en/nomenclature/LABRADOR-RETRIEVER-122.html

Gee, N. R., Church, M. T., & Altobelli, C. L. (2010). Preschoolers make fewer errors on an object categorization task in the presence of a dog. *Anthrozoös. 23*(3): 223–30.

Gee, N. R., Gould, J. K., Swanson, C. C., & Wagner, A. K. (2012). Preschoolers categorize animate objects better in the presence of a dog. *Anthrozoös. 25*(2), 187–198.

Gerritsen, R., & Haak, R. (2021). K9 professional tracking: A complete manual for theory and training. Brush Education Inc.

Haak, R. (1985). Portret van de Labrador Retriever. A.W. Bruna.

Haak, R. (1988). *Labrador Retriever.* Zuid-Hollandsche Uitgeversmaatschappij. Weert.

Halperin, M. (2002). Clinton names new dog Seamus: "It's a Chocolate Lab named Seamus." Politics. ABC News. 2 June.

Harding, T. (2018). Famous Amos: Therapy dog a hit at Plumb Library. *Sippican Week.* 28 January. https://sippican.theweektoday.com/node/32263

Harper, C. M., Dong, Y., Thornhill, T. S., Wright, J., Ready, J. Brick, G. W., & Dyer, G.. (2014). Can therapy dogs improve pain and satisfaction after total joint arthroplasty? A randomized controlled trial. *Clinical Orthopaedics and Related Research, 473*(1), 372–79.

Hawker, Lt. Col. P. (1814). *Instructions to young sportsmen, with directions for the choice, care, and management of guns; hints for the preservation of game; and instructions for shooting wildfowl. To which is added, a concise abridgment of the principal game laws.* J. Johnson and Co.

Hawkes, E. W. (1916). *The Labrador Eskimo.* Anthropological Series, Geological Survey, Ottawa, Memoir 91, No. 14. Reprinted in 1970 by the Johnson Reprint Corp.

Heady, B., Grabka, M., Kelley, J., Reddy, P., & Tseng, Y.-P. (2002). Pet ownership is good for your health and saves public expenditure too. Australian and German longitudinal evidence. *Australian Social Monitor, 5,* 93–99.

Hill, F. W. (1949). Sandylands. *Our Dogs Annual*, Manchester.

Hill, F. W. (1960). *Labradors*. (Foyles Handbooks), Foyle.

Howe, L. Countess. (1957). *The popular Labrador Retriever*. Popular Dogs Publishing Co. Ltd.

Hutchinson, W. N. (1869). *Dog breaking: The most expeditious, certain, and easy method*. John Murray.

James, H. (1910). A master's hand. *Country Life*. 12 November.

Jardine, W. (1840). *The naturalist's library: Volume 19*. In C. H. Smith, Mammalia; Dogs, Vol. 2, W. H. Lizars.

Johnson, R. A., & Meadows, R. L. (2010). Dog-walking: Motivation for adherence to a walking program. *Clinical Nursing Research, 19*(4), 387–402.

Jury, A. W. (1996). *Labrador Retrievers*. Crowood Press.

Kalmus, H. (1955). The discrimination by the nose of the dog of individual human odours and in particular of the odours of twins. *British Journal of Animal Behaviour, 5*, 25–31.

Kerss, J. S. (1896). Labrador dogs, *The Field*, 30 May.

King, E. J., Becker, F. R., & Markee, J. E. (1964). Studies on olfactory discrimination in dogs: (3) Ability to detect human odour trace. *Animal Behaviour, 12*, 311–315.

Kirton, A., Winter, A., Wirrell, E., & Snead, O. C. (2008). Seizure response dogs: Evaluation of a formal training program. *Epilepsy Behavior, 13*(3), 499–504. doi:10.1016/j.yebeh.2008.05.011

Kirton, A., Wirrell, E., Zhang, J., & Hamiwka, L. (2004). Seizure-alerting and -response behaviors in dogs living with epileptic children. *Neurology, 62*(12), 2303–5. doi:10.1212/wnl.62.12.2303

Komar, D. (1999). The use of cadaver dogs in locating scattered, scavenged human remains: Preliminary field test results. *Journal of Forensic Science, 44*(2), 405–8.

Krall, K. (1912). *Denkende Tiere, Beitrage zur Tierseelenkunde auf Grund Eigener Versuche, der Kluge Hans und Meine Pferde Muhamed und Zarif*. Friedrich Engelman.

Krauss, G. L., Choi, J. S., & Lesser, R. P. (2007). Pseudoseizure dogs. *Neurology, 68*(4), 308–309. doi:10.1212/01.wnl.0000250345.23677.6b

Lindsay, S. W., Pinder, M., Squires, C., Doggett, M., Kasstan, B. J., Hampshire, K., Kandeh, B., Dewhirst, S., Loga, J. G., D'Alessandro, U., & Guest, C. (2018). New study reports dogs successfully diagnosed malaria by sniffing socks worn by African children. Study presented at the American Society of Tropical Medicine and Hygiene (ASTMH) Annual Meeting, 29 October, New Orleans.

Lippi, G., & Cervellin, G. (2012). Canine olfactory detection of cancer versus laboratory testing: Myth or opportunity? *Clinical Chemistry and Laboratory Medicine, 50*(3), 435–9. doi: 10.1515/CCLM.2011.672

Los, E. A., Ramsey, K. L., Guttmann-Bauman, I., & Ahmann, A. J. (2017). Reliability of trained dogs to alert to hypoglycemia in patients with Type

1 diabetes. *Journal of Diabetes Science and Technology, 11*(3), 506–512. doi:10.1177/1932296816666537

Marcus, D. A., Bernstein, C. D., Constantin, J. M., Kunkel, F. A., Breuer, P., & Hanlon, R. B. (2013). Impact of animal-assisted therapy for outpatients with fibromyalgia. *Pain Medicine, 14*(1), 43–51.

Martijn, C. J., Barkham, S., & Barkham, M. M. (2003). Basques? Beothuk? Innu? Inuit? or St. Lawrence Iroquoians? The whalers on the 1546 Desceliers Map, seen through the eyes of different beholders. *Newfoundland and Labrador Studies, 19*(1).

McCulloch, M., Jezierski, T., Broffman, M., Hubbard, A., Turner, K., & Janecki, T. (2006). Diagnostic accuracy of canine scent detection in early- and late-stage lung and breast cancers. *Integrated Cancer Therapy, 5*(1), 30–9.

McCulloch, M., Turner, K., & Broffman, M. (2012). Lung cancer detection by canine scent: Will there be a lab in the lab? *European Respiratory Journal, 39*, 511–512.

Miklósi, Á., Polgárdi, R., Topál, J., & Csányi, V. (1998). Use of experimenter-given cues in dogs. *Animal Cognition, 1*, 113–121.

Miner, R. J.-T. (2001). The experience of living with and using a guide dog. *RE:view, 32*(4), 183–90. https://eric.ed.gov/?id=EJ623128

O'Haire, M. E., McKenzie, S. J., Beck, A. M., & Slaughter, V. (2013). Social behaviors increase in children with autism in the presence of animals compared to toys. *PLoS ONE, 8*(2). doi:10.1371/journal.pone.0057010

O'Haire, M. E., & Rodriguez, K. E. (2018). Preliminary efficacy of service dogs as a complementary treatment for posttraumatic stress disorder in military members and veterans. *Journal of Consulting and Clinical Psychology, 86*(2), 179–188.

Parker, E. (Ed.). (1929). *Shooting by moor, field and shore*. (The Lonsdale Library, Volume III). Seeley, Service.

Pastore, R. T. (1998). *Aboriginal Peoples*. Heritage Newfoundland & Labrador. https://www.heritage.nf.ca/toc/aboriginal-peoples-table-of-contents.php#relpre

Pfungst, O. (1911). *Clever Hans. The horse of Mr. Von Osten*. Holt, Rinehart & Winston.

Pickel, D. P., Manucy, G. P., Walker, D. B., Hall, S. B., & Walker, J. C. (2004). Evidence for canine olfactory detection of melanoma. *Applied Animal Behavior Science, 4*(89),107–116.

Rodriguez, K. E., Bryce, C. I., Granger, D. A., & O'Haire, M. E. (2018). The effect of a service dog on salivary cortisol awakening response in a military population with posttraumatic stress disorder (PTSD). *Psychoneuroendocrinology, 98*, 202–210. https://doi.org/10.1016/j.psyneuen.2018.04.026

Roslin-Williams, M. (1969). *The Dual-purpose Labrador*. Pelham Books.

Saint-Hilaire, G., & Cuvier, F. (1824). *Histoire Naturelle des Mammifères*. (Volume I). Chez A. Belin Libraire Editeur

Saunders, G. H., Biswas, K., Serpi, T., McGovern, S., Groer, S., Stock, E. M., & McCranie, M. (2017). Design and challenges for a randomized, multi-site clinical trial comparing the use of service dogs and emotional support dogs in veterans with post-traumatic stress disorder (PTSD). *Contemporary Clinical Trials, 62*, 105–113.

Schoon, G. A. A. (1997). The performance of dogs in identifying humans by scent. Thesis, University of Leiden, The Netherlands.

Schoon, G. A. A. (1998). A first assessment of the reliability of an improved scent identification line-up. *Journal of Forensic Sciences, 43*(1), 70–75.

Schoon, G. A. A., & Haak, R. (2002). *K9 suspect discrimination: Training and practicing scent identification line-ups*. Detselig Enterprises.

Scott, Lord G., & Middleton, Sir J. (1936). *The Labrador dog*. Witherby.

Settle, R. H., Sommerville, B. A., McCormick, J., & Broom, D. M. (1994). Human scent matching using specially trained dogs. *Animal Behavior, 48*, 1443–1448.

Shaw, V. (1881). *The illustrated book of the dog*. Cassell, Petter, Galpin & Co.

Sherwinski, A. (2018). *Joplin Public Library gets surprise visit from therapy dogs*. Four States home page. 30 January. https://www.fourstateshomepage.com/news/joplin-public-library-gets-surprise-visit-from-therapy-dogs/946335825

Sobo, E. J., Eng, B., & Kassity-Krich, N. (2006). Canine visitation (pet) therapy: Pilot study data on decrease in child pain perception. *Journal of Holistic Nursing, 24*, 51–57.

Sommerville, B. A., Green, M. A., & Gee, D. J. (1990). Using chromatography and a dog to identify some of the compounds in human sweat which are under genetic influence. In D. W. MacDonald, D. Müller-Schwarz, & S. E. Natynczuk (Eds.), *Chemical Signals in Vertebrates 5*, Oxford University Press, 634-639.

Sonoda, H., Kohnoe, S., Yamazato, T., Satoh, Y., Morizono, G., Shikata, K., Morita, M., Watanabe, A., Morita M., Kakeji, Y., Inoue, F., & Maehara, Y. (2011). Colorectal cancer screening with odour material by canine scent detection. *Gut, 60*(6), 814–819. https://doi.org/10.1136/gut.2010.218305

Soproni, K., Miklósi, Á., Topál, J., & Csányi, V. (2001). Comprehension of human communicative signs in pet dogs *(Canis familiaris). Journal of Comparative Psychology, 115*(2), 122–126.

Sprake, L. (1933). *The Labrador Retriever: Its history, points and training*. Witherby.

St. John, C. (1849). *A tour in Sutherlandshire, with extracts from the field books of a sportsman and naturalist*. (Volume 2). John Murray.

Stonehenge (pseudonym of John Henry Walsh). (1867). *The dog in health and disease*. Longmans, Green, Reader and Dyer.

Strong, V., Brown, S., & Walker, R. (1999). Seizure-alert dogs—fact or fiction? *Seizure, 8*(1), 62–5. doi:10.1053/seiz.1998.0250

Taplin, W. (1803). *Sportsman's cabinet*. Printed for the proprietors. London

The Kennel Club. (2019). *Labrador Retriever breed standard*. https://www.thekennelclub.org.uk/breed-standards/gundog/retriever-labrador/

Tuck, J. A. (1976.) *Newfoundland and Labrador prehistory*. Canadian Museum of Civilization.

United Kennel Club. (2019). *Labrador Retriever breed standard*. https://www.ukcdogs.com/labrador-retriever

Warwick, H. (1964). *The complete Labrador Retriever*. Howell Book House.

Westfall, S. (2010). *An early depiction of a yellow retriever*. Natural History website. 9 December. https://retrieverman.net/tag/early-yellow-retriever/

Westfall, S. (2011). *Lambert De Boilieu on the "Labrador dog."* Natural History website. 1 April. https://retrieverman.net/2011/04/01/lambert-de-boilieu-on-the-labrador-dog/

Westfall, S. (2011). *Charles St. John on water Retrievers*. Natural History website. 24 April. https://retrieverman.net/2011/04/24/charles-st-john-on-water-retrievers/

Whitmarsh, L. (2005). The benefits of guide dog ownership. *Visual Impairment Research, 7*(1), 27–42. doi:10.1080/13882350590956439

Williams, H., & Pembroke, A. (1989). Sniffer dogs in the melanoma clinic? *Lancet, 1*, 734.

Willis, C. M., Church, S. M., Guest, C. M., Cook, W. A., McCarthy, N., Bransbury, A. J., et al. (2004). Olfactory detection of human bladder cancer by dogs: A proof of principle study. *BMJ, 329*, 712–4.

Wolters, R. A. (1981). *The Labrador Retriever. The history…the people*. Peterson Prints.

Notes

CHAPTER 1

1. B. Clarke. (1981). *Inuit in Labrador,* Museum notes published on The Rooms Provincial Museum website, https://www.therooms.ca/inuit-in-labrador
2. Stonehenge (pseudonym of John Henry Walsh). (1867). *The dog in health and disease,* (Longmans, Green, Reader and Dyer).
3. Countess L. Howe. (1957). *The popular Labrador Retriever*. Popular Dogs Publishing Co. Ltd.
4. W. E. Cormack. (1873). *Narrative of a journey across the island of Newfoundland.*
5. C. W. E. St. John. (1849). *A tour in Sutherlandshire, with extracts from the field-books of a sportsman and naturalist,* (Volume 2), John Murray.
6. S. Westfall. (2011). *Charles St. John on water Retrievers,* Natural History website, 24 April, https://retrieverman.net/2011/04/24/charles-st-john-on-water-retrievers/
7. L. de Boilieu. (1861). *Recollections of Labrador life*. Saunders, Otley, & Co., 172–173.
8. De Boilieu. *Recollections of Labrador life,* 239–244.
9. S. Westfall. (2011). *Lambert de Boilieu on the "Labrador dog,"* Natural History website, 1 April, https://retrieverman.net/2011/04/01/lambert-de-boilieu-on-the-labrador-dog/

CHAPTER 2

1. Lt. Col. P. Hawker. (1814). *Instructions to young sportsmen, with directions for the choice, care, and management of guns; hints for the preservation of game; and instructions for shooting wildfowl. To which is added, a concise abridgment of the principal game laws.* J. Johnson and Co.
2. J. S. Kerss. (1896). Labrador dogs, *The Field,* 30 May.
3. V. Shaw. (1881). *The illustrated book of the dog*. Cassell, Petter, Galpin & Co.
4. H. James. (1910). A master's hand, *Country Life,* 12 November.
5. D. Cairns. (1912). The Hon. A. Holland-Hibbert's Labradors, *Country Life,* 3 August.
6. Ibid.
7. Ibid.
8. Peter of Faskally wins the Open Retriever Stakes in the Perthshire Dog Trials, *Dundee Courier* (28 October 1910).
9. Kennel Club Challenge Cup, *The Field* (18 November 1911).
10. The Retriever Championship, *The Field* (25 November 1911).
11. Maj. M. Portal in Eric Parker (Ed.). (1929). *Shooting by moor, field and shore,* (The Lonsdale Library, Volume III), Seeley, Service.

12. Countess L. Howe. (1957). *The popular Labrador Retriever*. Popular Dogs Publishing Co.
13. G. Broadley. (1968). *The Retriever owner's encyclopaedia*. Pelham Books.
14. R. Edwards. (2005). *Sandylands: An historical perspective*. Sandylands.net, http://www.sandylands.net/history2.html
15. F. W. Hill. (1949), Sandylands, *Our dogs annual,* Manchester.
16. R. Edwards. *Sandylands*.
17. Ibid.
18. D. Craig. (2008). *The Labrador Retriever*, (Best of Breed Series), Magnet & Steel.
19. M. Halperin. (2002). Clinton names new dog Seamus: "It's a Lab named Seamus." Politics. (ABC News, 2 June).
20. Scottie Westfall, (2010). *An early depiction of a yellow Retriever,* Natural History website, 9 December, https://retrieverman.net/tag/early-yellow-retriever/

CHAPTER 3

1. **American Kennel Club breed standard:** http://images.akc.org/pdf/breeds/standards/LabradorRetriever.pdf; **Canadian Kennel Club breed standards:** https://www.ckc.ca/en/Files/Breed-Standards/Breed-Standards/Group-1-Sporting-Dogs; **The Kennel Club breed standard:** https://www.thekennelclub.org.uk/services/public/breed/standard.aspx?id=2048; **Fédération Cynologique Internationale breed standard:** http://www.fci.be/en/nomenclature/LABRADOR-RETRIEVER-122.html; **United Kennel Club breed standard:** https://www.ukcdogs.com/labrador-retriever

CHAPTER 4

1. O. Pfungst. (1911). *Clever Hans. The horse of Mr. Von Osten*, Holt, Rinehart & Winston.
2. K. Krall. (1912). *Denkende Tiere, Beitrage zur Tierseelenkunde auf Grund Eigener Versuche, der Kluge Hans und Meine Pferde Muhamed und Zarif*, Friedrich Engelman.
3. A. Miklósi, R. Polgárdi, J. Topál, & V. Csányi. (1998). Use of experimenter-given cues in dogs, *Animal Cognition, 1,* 113–121.
    K. Soproni, A. Miklósi, J. Topál, & V. Csányi, (2001). Comprehension of human communicative signs in pet dogs *(Canis familiaris), Journal of Comparative Psychology, 115*(2), 122–126.

CHAPTER 5

1. Champion Retrievers. (1910). *Country Life,* 12 November, 694–696.
2. E. C. Ash. (1927). *Dogs: Their history and development*. Houghton Mifflin Co., 376.

CHAPTER 6

1. A. F. Abdel Fattah, & H. S. A. Gharib. (2020). Investigation police dog olfactory acuity through: Comparing various dog breeds, previous training experiences and searching site on the detection of narcotics, *Advances in Animal Veterinary Science, 8*(s2), 58–63. http://dx.doi.org/10.17582/journal.aavs/2020/8.s2.58.63
2. More information can be found in our book *K9 investigation errors: A manual for avoiding mistakes* (2016, Brush Education).

Photo Credits

Unless otherwise stated below, all figures are from the archives of the authors.

Belgian federal police: 6.17–6.20 (www.polfed-fedpol.becia/gov); **Colourbox:** 6.12 (809987), 6.13 (1196630); **Freepik.com:** 4.2; *Onze Hond* **magazine photo archive:** 2.29–2.31, 2.32–2.34, 4.7, 5.10–5.12, 5.14, 6.22, 6.23, 7.1, 7.3, 7.4, 7.8, 7.10; **The Rooms Provincial Archives Division, Newfoundland and Labrador:** 1.4, 1.7; **Shutterstock:** 6.5 (Micimakin); **Wikimedia Commons:** 0.1 (Blaine Hansel), 0.3 (Giuseppe Pitzus), 0.4 (Mattias Agar), 0.5 (Gunnandreassen), 0.6 (Nevilley), 0.7 (Cal119), 0.8 (Dirk Vorderstraße), 1.1 (Nilfanion), 3.2 (Erikeltic), 3.3 (mcclave), 4.1 (Losch), 4.3 (IDS.photos), 4.4 (Elf), 4.5 (Losch), 4.6 (IDS.photos), 4.7 (Losch), 4.11 (Teamlabrador), 4.12 (Joseph Carr), 4.16 (Rronenow), 4.19 (Ltshears), 4.20 (Mhawky), 4.21 (IDS.photos), 4.23 (Peckinpah), 4.24 (Ian Kirk), 5.8 (Albert de Muyser), 5.9 (Herwig Kavallar), 5.13 (Sarobaxana), 5.15 (Cali1008), 5.16 (Madeleine Lewander), 5.17 (Giuseppe Pitzus), 6.1 (Jami430), 6.2 (Sgt. Kent Redmond), 6.3 (Zipster969/ Master Sgt. Cohen Young), 6.4 (Pete Markham), 6.6 (Lance Cpl. Derrick K. Irions), 6.7 (kngf), 6.8 (kngf), 6.9 (Zipster969/ pawsitivityservicedogs.com), 6.10 (Zipster969), 6.11 (Zipster969/ pawsitivityservicedogs.com), 6.16 (tinbotu), 6.21 (State Farm), 7.2 (Cpl. Joshua Young), 7.5 (Askolnick), 7.6 (Cpl. Reece Lodder, US Marine Corps), 7.9 (soldiersmediacenter, US Air Force photo/Staff Sgt. Stacy L. Pearsall)

About the Authors

Ruud Haak is the author of more than 30 dog books in Dutch and German. Over 40 years he has been the editor-in-chief of the biggest Dutch dog magazine, *Onze Hond* (*Our Dog*). He was born in 1947 in Amsterdam, the Netherlands. At the age of 13, he was training police dogs at his uncle's security dog training center, and when he was 15, he worked after school with his patrol dog (which he trained himself) at the Amsterdam harbor. He later started training his dogs in Schutzhund and IGP, and he successfully bred and showed German shepherds and Saint Bernards.

Ruud worked as a social therapist in a government clinic for criminal psychopaths. From his studies in psychology, he became interested in dog behavior and training methods for nose work, especially the tracking dog and the search-and-rescue dog. More

Ruud Haak with his German Shepherd Yes van Sulieseraad and Malinois Google van het Eldenseveld.

Resi Gerritsen with her Malinois Halusetha's All Power and Malinois Google van het Eldenseveld.

recently he has trained drug- and explosive-detector dogs for the Dutch police and the Royal Dutch Airforce. He is also a visiting lecturer at Dutch, German, and Austrian police-dog schools.

In the 1970s, Ruud and his wife, Dr. Resi Gerritsen, a psychologist and jurist, attended many courses and symposia with their German shepherds for Schutzhund, tracking dog, and search-and-rescue dog training in Switzerland, Germany, and Austria. In 1979, they started the Dutch Rescue Dog Organization in the Netherlands. With that unit, they attended many operations responding to earthquakes, gas explosions, and lost persons in wooded or wilderness areas. In 1990, Ruud and Resi moved to Austria, where they were asked by the Austrian Red Cross to select and train operational rescue and avalanche dogs. They lived for three years at a height of 6,000 feet (1800 m) in the Alps and worked with their dogs in search missions after avalanches.

With their Austrian colleagues, Ruud and Resi developed a new method for training search-and-rescue dogs. This way of training showed the best results after a major earthquake in Armenia (1988), an earthquake in Japan (1995), two major earthquakes in Turkey (1999), and big earthquakes in Algeria and Iran (2003). Ruud and Resi have also demonstrated the success of their unique training methods for tracking dogs as well as search-and-rescue dogs at the Austrian, Czech, Hungarian, and World Championships, where both were several times the leading champions.

Resi and Ruud have held many symposia and master classes all over the world on their unique training methods, which are featured in their books:

- *K9 Complete Care: A Manual for Physically and Mentally Healthy Working Dogs*
- *K9 Drug Detection: A Manual for Training and Operations*
- *K9 Explosive and Mine Detection: A Manual for Training and Operations*
- *K9 Investigation Errors and How to Avoid Them*
- *K9 Personal Protection: A Manual for Training Reliable Protection Dogs*
- *K9 Professional Tracking: A Complete Manual for Theory and Training*
- *K9 Scent Training: A Manual for Training Your Identification, Tracking, and Detection Dog*
- *K9 Schutzhund: A Manual for IGP Training through Positive Reinforcement*
- *K9 Search and Rescue: A Manual for Training the Natural Way*
- *K9 Working Breeds: Characteristics and Capabilities*
- *The German Shepherd: A Historical View of the Breed's Development, Prime, and Deterioration*
- *The Malinois: The History and Development of the Breed in Schutzhund, Detection and Police Work*

With Simon Prins they wrote *K9 Behavior Basics: A Manual for Proven Success in Operational Service Dog Training*; and with Dr. Adee Schoon, Ruud wrote *K9 Suspect Discrimination: Training and Practicing Scent Identification Line-Ups*. All of these books were published by Detselig Enterprises Ltd., Calgary, Canada (now Brush Education Inc.).

Ruud and Resi now live in the Netherlands. They are international judges for the International Search and Rescue Dog Organisation (IRO) and the Fédération Cynologique Internationale (FCI). Ruud and Resi are still successfully training their dogs as detector dogs for search and rescue, drugs, explosives, and Schutzhund. You can contact the authors by email at resigerritsen@gmail.com.